Ryoko Yojin Shu

旅行用心集

How to Travel Safely in Japan
Published in Edo 1810

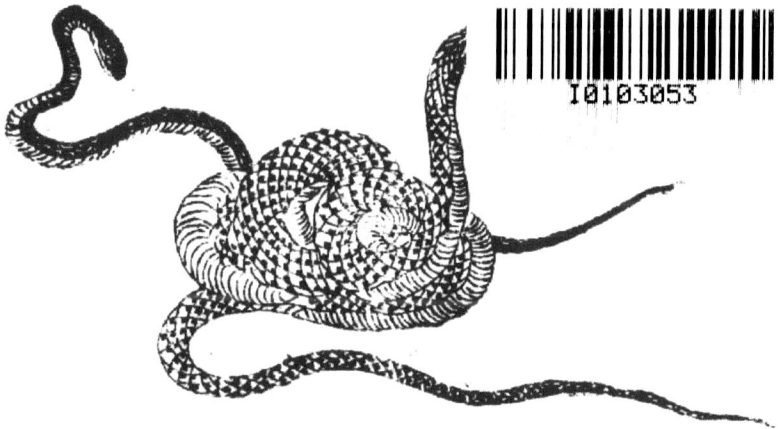

I0103053

八隅蘆菴著
By Yasumi Roan

シャハン・エリック訳
Translated by Eric Shahan

YASUMI ROAN・八隅蘆菴

西華　　　東泰

中嵩

南衡　　　北恒

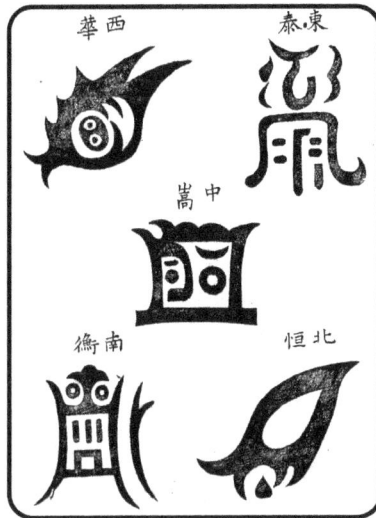

Translator's Introduction

How to Travel Safely in Japan contains quite a few illustrations. However, while translating, I had to refer to several other Edo Era travel books to accurately translate the text. Several of the books I used for reference contained illustrations that show the scenery and stops along the official roads traversing Japan, in addition to the different modes of travel. I have included them to help visualize what travel was like in the early 19th century and also to show how areas looked in the past.

Illustrations not originally included in *How to Travel Safely in Japan* will have the source cited below the illustration and will be surrounded with a box. If there is no citation it is from *How to Travel Safely in Japan*.

In addition, I was able to locate examples of the documents and permits discussed in this book, and translated them into English for the first time.

文化七庚午年秋新開彫

旅行用心集 全

Ryoko Yojinshu Zen
Traveling Safely in Japan : One Volume

Engraved the beginning of Autumn of Bunka 7 (1810)

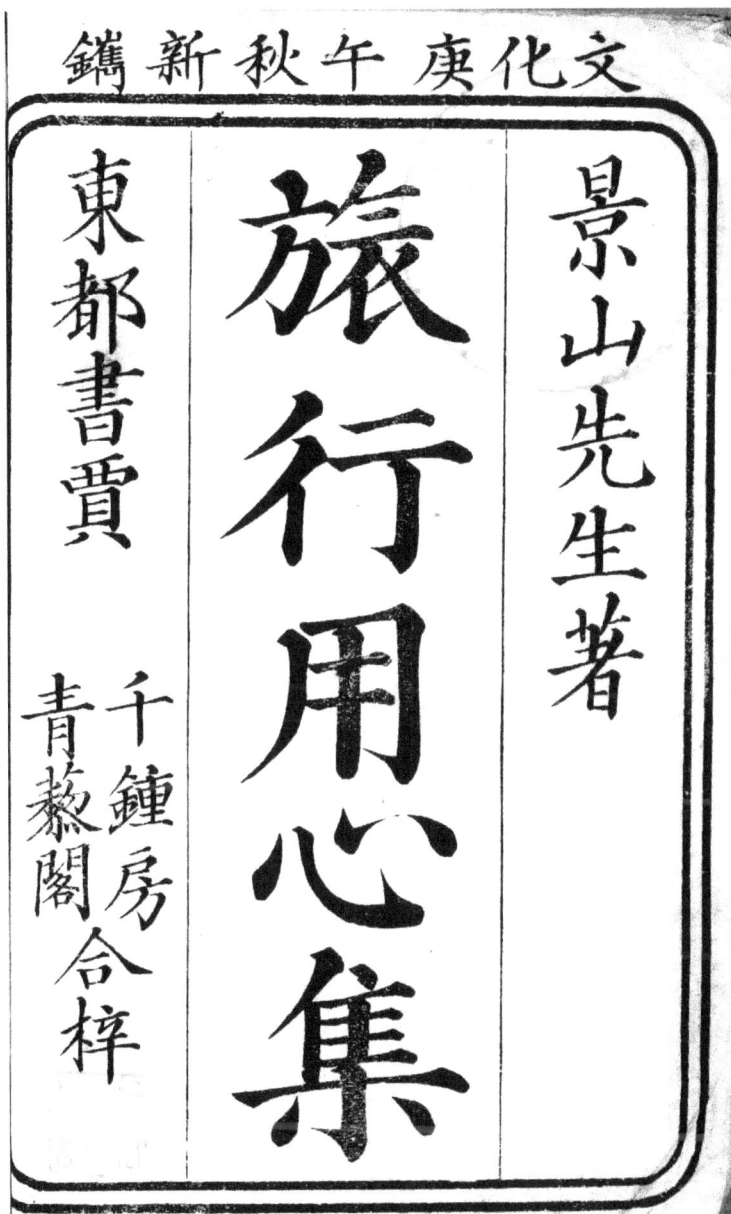

文化庚午秋新鐫

景山先生著

旅行用心集

東都書賈

千鍾房
青藜閣合梓

Traveling Safely in Japan
New Edition Bunka 7 (1810)
By Kage-yama Sensei (Yasumi Roan)

Introduction

Maybe you want to take time off from work to visit Ise Grand Shrine in Mie Prefecture, or maybe someone has invited you to accompany them on a trip. At some point you will decide, "Alright then, on the next auspicious day I will set out." You will receive farewell gifts from all manner of people and your household will be bustling with excited energy as everyone helps with your preparations. A quite enjoyable time indeed.

When the day of your departure finally arrives, it will not just be your family that sees you off, rather the whole village will send you on your way. Cups of sake will be passed back and forth as various people give you advice like, "Be careful of this!" or "Watch out for that!" While this advice is well-intentioned, it is given to cover up how envious they are of your trip.

Even if you are departing on a business trip or some official duty, no matter your age, you will swell with anticipation and your whole body will feel energized.

If you live in eastern Japan you will no doubt be traveling to Ise Grand Shrine, Yamato, Kyoto, Osaka, Shikoku, Kyushu and so on.

Those living in western Japan will be hoping to visit Ise Shrine before traveling to Edo, Kashima, Katori, Nikko, Oshu Matsu Shima, Kisagata and Shinshu Zenkoji.[1]

---

[1] The following pages will give a brief introduction to these famous places which would have been well-known to Japanese people.

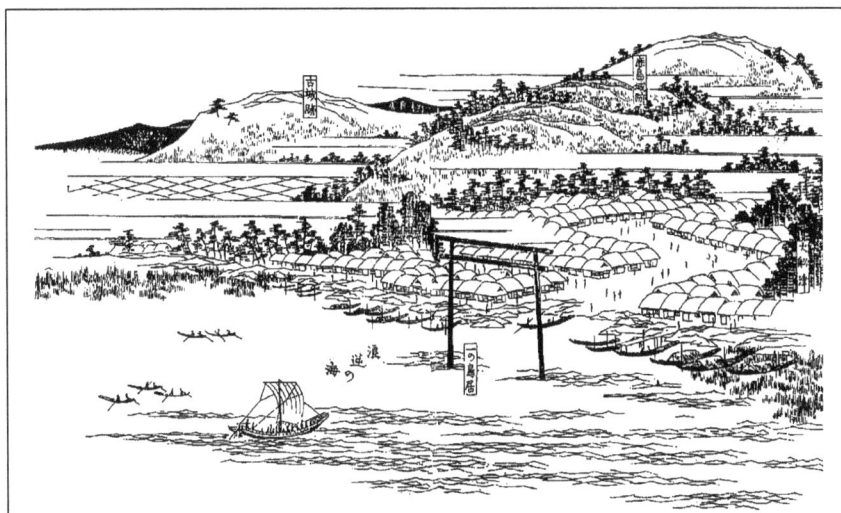

Kashima 鹿島 refers to Kashima Jingu Shrine 鹿島神宮 in Ibaraki Prefecture. The foundation of Kashima Jingu Shrine predates the historical record, but legend states it was founded in 600 BC. The illustration above is the entrance to Kashima town from the north. The mound on the back left is the ruins of Kashima Castle.

Illustration of a nighttime celebration that is a mix of both Buddhist and Shinto religions. From *Essence of Kashima* 鹿島志 published in 1824.

The Ise Grand Shrine 伊勢神宮 Ise Jingū from the Edo Era
Famous Illustrations of Ise Grand Shrine 伊勢参宮名所図会
The Ise Grand Shrine is in Mie Prefecture and is dedicated to the
sun goddess Amaterasu. It is one of the oldest Shinto shrines.

During the Edo period it was popular to do the *Okage Mairi* お蔭参り, or secret pilgrimage. This ceremony occurred roughly 3 times every 60 years. It was famous because Samurai would leave without notice and children would run away from home to visit the shrine. Since so many people would skip out on work it was also known as *Nuke Mairi* 抜け参り Skipping Work Pilgrimage.

Katori 香取日光 refers to Katori Jingu Shrine 香取神宮 in Chiba Prefecture.   The foundation of Katori Shrine predates the historical period but legend states it was founded in 643 BC.

香取大神宮

Illustration from *Illustrated Guide to Famous Sites in Edo* 江戸名所図会 Published 1830's. By Saito Yukio 斎藤幸雄 (1737-1799) and Hasegawa Settan.長谷川雪旦 (1778-1843)

Nikko 日光 is a town in Tochigi Prefecture famous for Toshogu, the shrine and mausoleum of Tokugawa Ieyasu, the founder of the Tokugawa Shogunate, which ruled Japan from 1600-1868. Illustration of a traveler enjoying one of the many waterfalls in the area. From *The Mt. Nikko Scroll* 日光山図巻 Edo Era. Author and artist unknown.

Illustration of *Urami no Taki* "Waterfall you can view from behind" in Nikko from *60 Famous Spots* 六十余州名所図会
By Utagawa Hiroshige 歌川広重
1850s

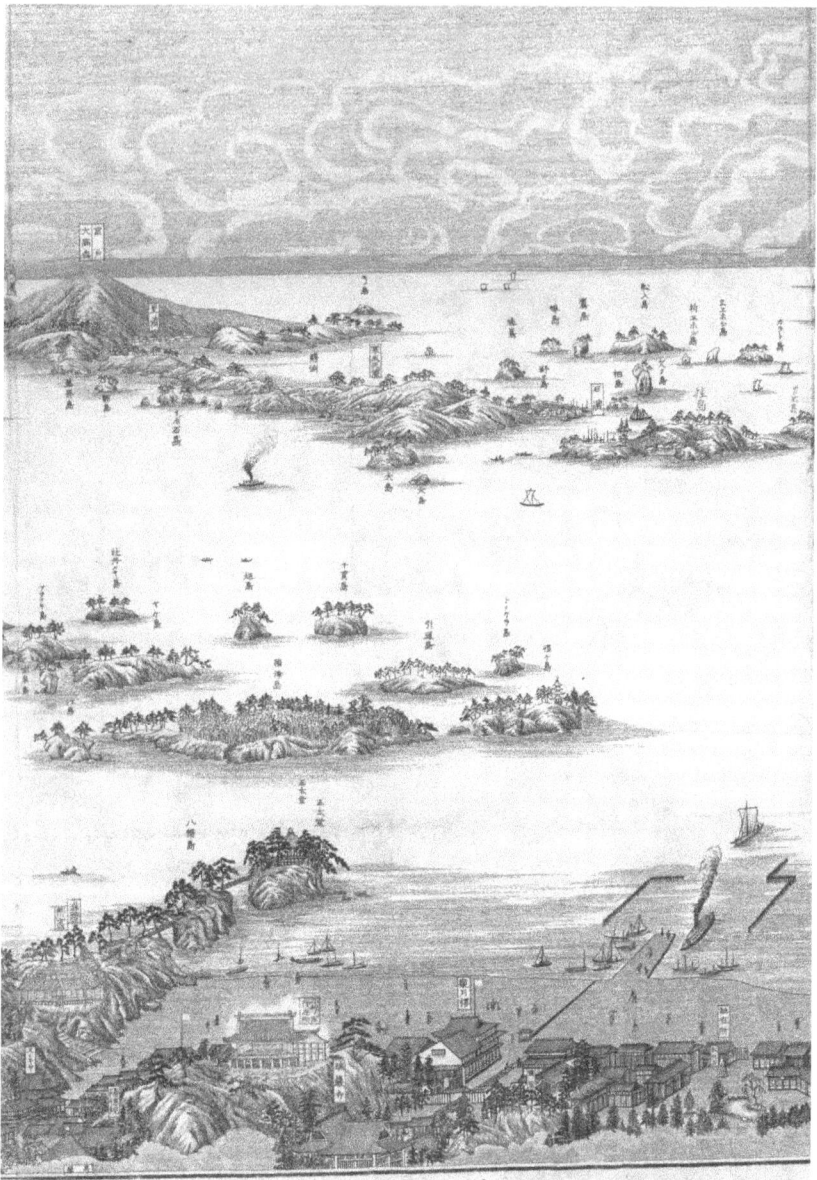

Oshu Matsu Shima 松島 is a group of 260 small islands near Miyagi Prefecture. The tiny islands are all covered with pines and the area is famous for one of the greatest scenery views in Japan.

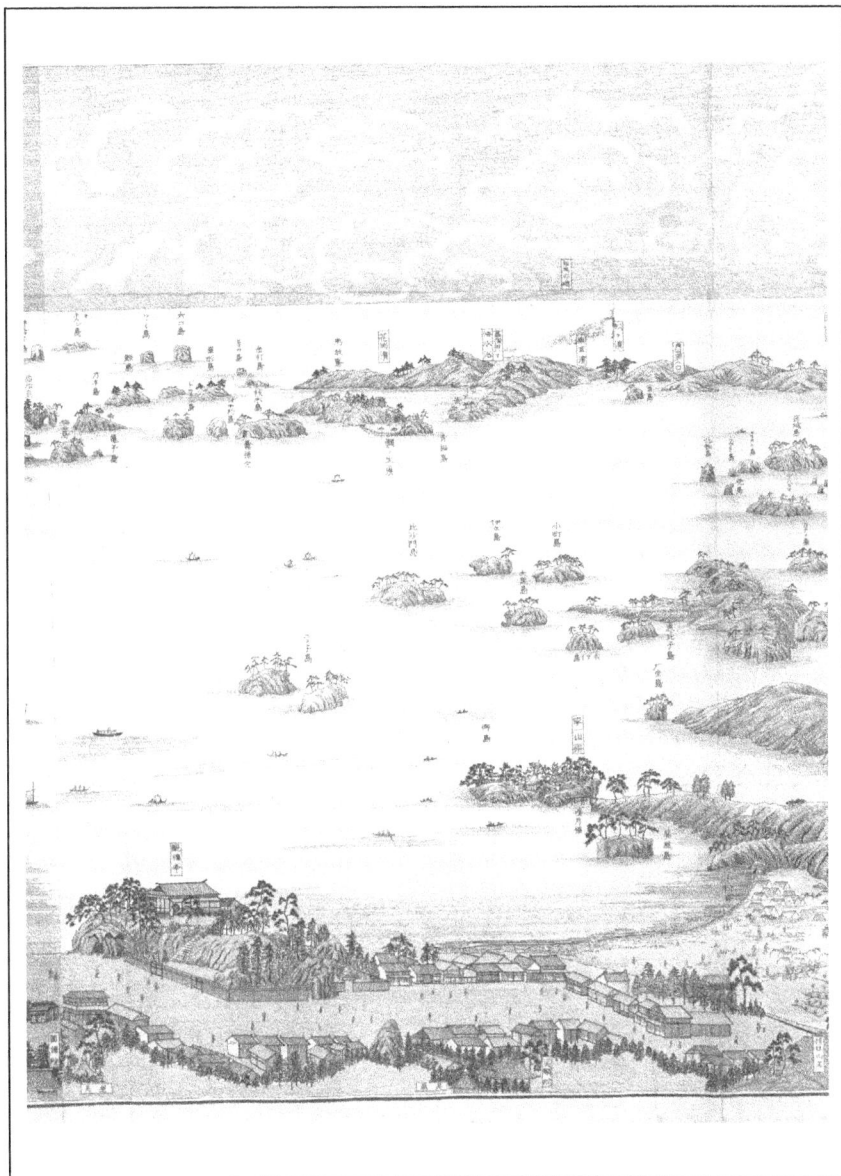

From: *New and Old Illustrations of Oshu Matsushima* 奥州松島
全島旧新三図附瑞巌寺図 Published 1810

Kisagata 象潟 was an inland lake that sported many small islands with pine trees growing on them. In 1804 an earthquake raised the ground enough so most of the floor of the lake was exposed and ensuing irrigation projects fully drained the lake.

Illustration from A Journey to Kisagata 象潟行 by Ri Kyo 里杏

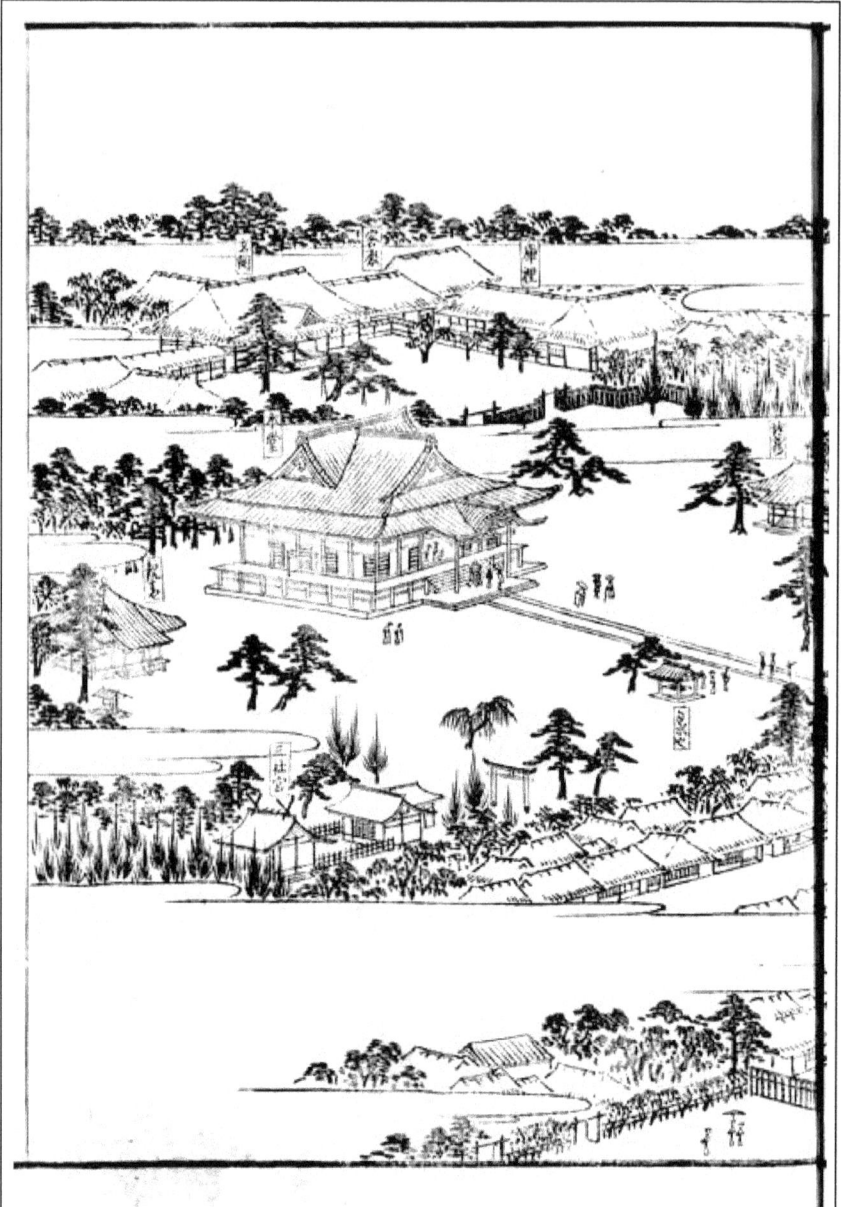

Zenkō-ji 善光寺 *Temple of the Benevolent Light* is a 7th century temple located in Nagano Prefecture.

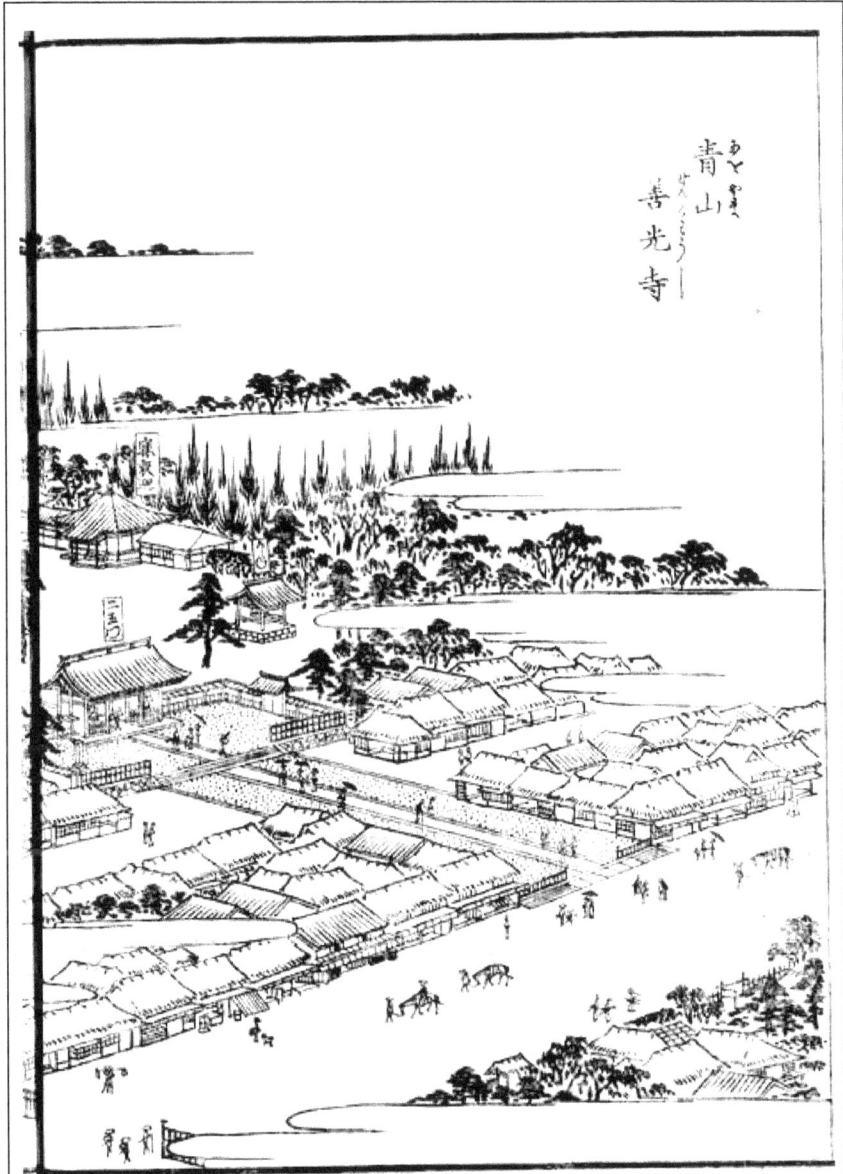

Illustration from *Illustrated Guide to Famous Sites in Edo* 江戸名所図会 Published 1830s. By Saito Yukio 斎藤幸雄 (1737-1799) and Hasegawa Settan.長谷川雪旦 (1778-1843)

The desire to travel is widespread, even if you are satisfied with your job and your family is happy and healthy. All over Japan people feel compelled to visit Ise Shrine at least once in their lives. Clearly, people like the lord of your domain and his retainers will make such a trip, but they will also bring their family members and relatives along. It is almost like a lesson learned at school.

Let me just say here that no matter what your status in society is, Samurai, Farmer, Craftsmen or Trader, if you work diligently every day you will never go hungry and you will be able to live your life peacefully and enjoyably. This is due to our devotion to the Shinto Gods and the Buddha.

Some people, though they are born into a wealthy family are stricken with an illness that leaves them sickly and weak. Such people, no matter how much they desire to travel are rendered unable to set out and gaze upon unique scenery, walk on trails or climb sacred mountains. Some readers are no doubt thinking, "Well if they have money they can hire a palanquin to carry them about." However, unfortunately this way of traveling would no doubt be disappointing. It is nearly as disappointing as a healthy but poor person who yearns to travel. A tragic state of affairs.

In the end it does not matter how much money you have, there is no greater blessing than being healthy enough to set out on a pilgrimage to a temple. There are several important things I would like travelers to remember after they embark on a journey. The first is to always take care of your own Matabiki pants, Zori sandals and other equipment. Even if you are traveling with other people, always take care of your own things.

Next, even if the breakfast or dinner at the place you are staying is not to your liking, eat a full meal every time. When traveling you should learn to not get frustrated when things don't go as planned. Consider adversity a chance to test yourself.[2]

Finally, depending on what area of Japan you are in, the customs and manners of people may be quite different from what you are used to and you may have a hard time adjusting. However, as I said before, just set those feeling aside and think, "That is just how they do things around here." This is the mindset you should keep.

While on the road many difficulties can arise. You may encounter wind and rain. Due to some unforeseeable reason, you may have to rise early to cross a mountain covered in thick fog or you may find yourself with only a thin futon to keep you warm at night. It is possible you may end up getting into a fight with someone in your group or another traveler or maybe your feet will begin to hurt so much you can no longer proceed. The changing weather could make an old illness to flare up. However, unlike when you are at home it can be quite difficult to get quick satisfactory treatment. In short, the trials and tribulations you will face while traveling across Japan are hard to put into words.

For this reason embarking on a trip is a great learning experience for young people. There is even an aphorism regarding this, *Send your treasured child out into the world.* Whether rich or poor, people who have not traveled have no idea about the hardships while on the road. Such a person considers a trip to be akin to a fun time having a picnic on the side of a mountain. These sorts of people are lacking in empathy and treat other people flippantly. In the end

---

[2] The author calls this *Shugyo*, intensive physical and spiritual training.

they are the kind of people that end up getting mocked behind their backs.

Unless there is a river that has become impassible due to a flood, everyone, even Daimyo, lords and royalty will have to put one foot in front of the other to reach their overnight accommodation. This could be in the middle of high winds and hard rain. Therefore, when traveling, there is no room for self-indulgent willful behavior from everyday people.

Anyone who goes on a journey will have to endure a great many hardships and learn to understand the customs and manners in many different places, which will serve to develop their empathy. Having developed this empathy those around will think you are a good person. The humanity you learn while on the road will assist you as you succeed in life and pass on what you have learned to your children and grandchildren. This is the true meaning of, *Send your treasured child out into the world.*

I have loved traveling since I was young and I ventured out on trips both near and far. Some of my acquaintances heard about my travels and began to consider me something of an expert and asked me innumerable questions. I used to write letters answering all their questions. Recently, as I've grown older, writing such letters has become troublesome. On the other hand, I do not wish to refuse to help anyone. Thus, I have gathered together all my notes on travel and reflected on my past journeys, I have set my thoughts to paper. As I feel this book will be helpful to those setting out on a journey I have called it *A Collection of Things to be Careful of When Traveling.*

Yasumi Roan
June 1810

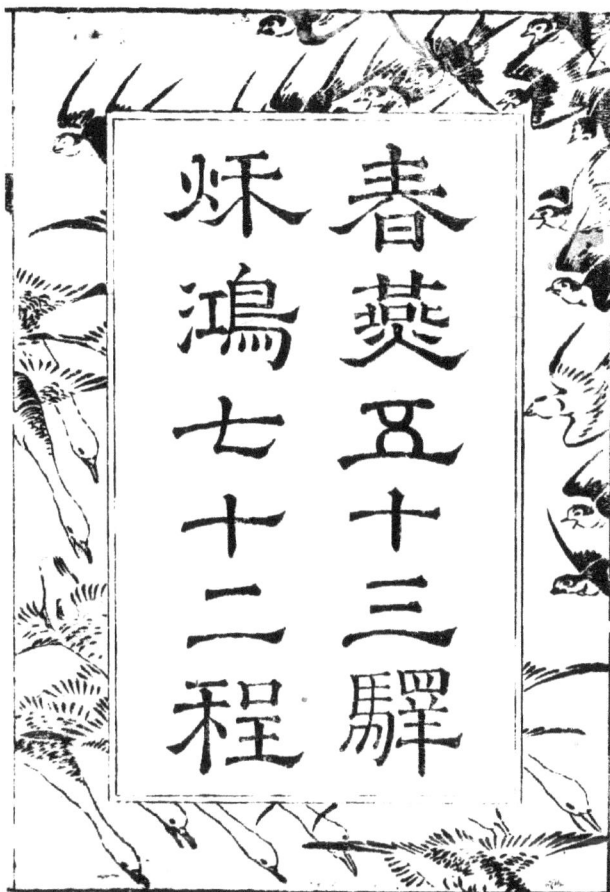

春燕五十三駅
Spring Tsubame 53 Stations
This is another name for the 53 Stations of the Tokaido Road.

秋鴻七十二程

Seventy-two types of weather, plants and animals that a wild goose encounters over the course of a year.[3]

---

[3] These two phrases use birds as their focus but together they call to mind an image of the changes in weather scenery, and wildlife a traveler will encounter while walking along the Tōkaidō or any other of Japan's Edo Era highways.

Table of Contents 1

26

Table of Contents 2

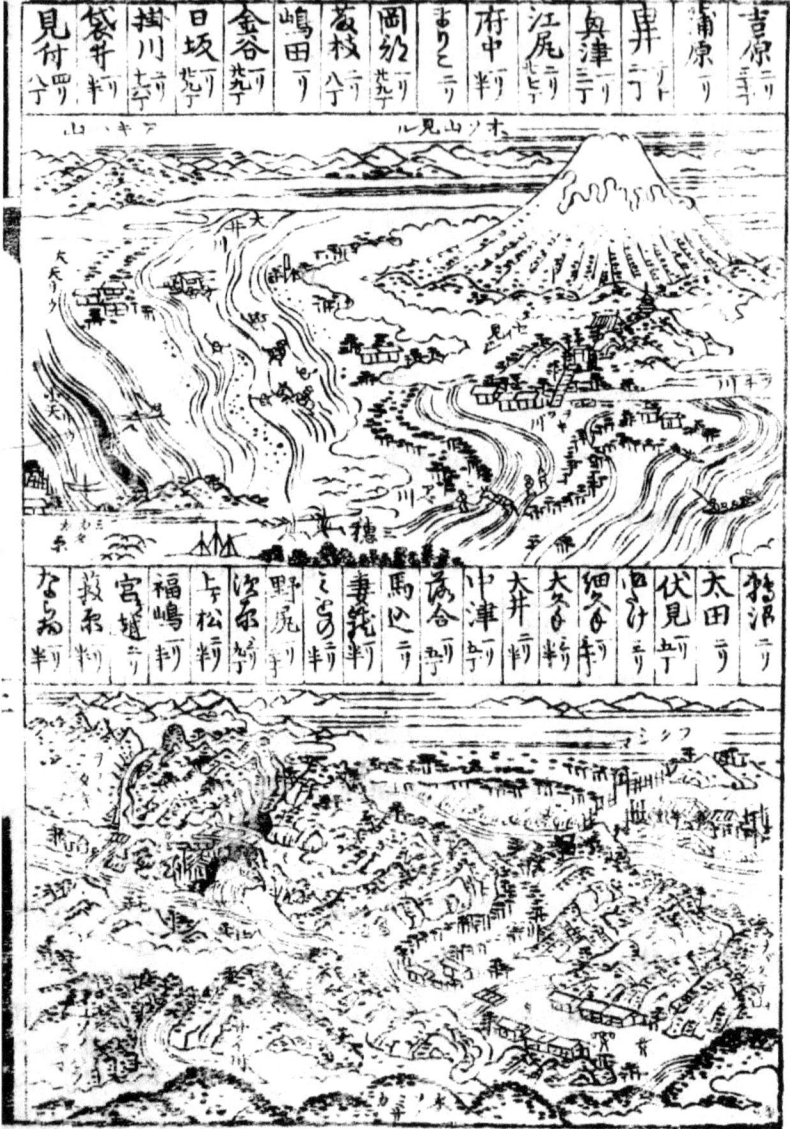

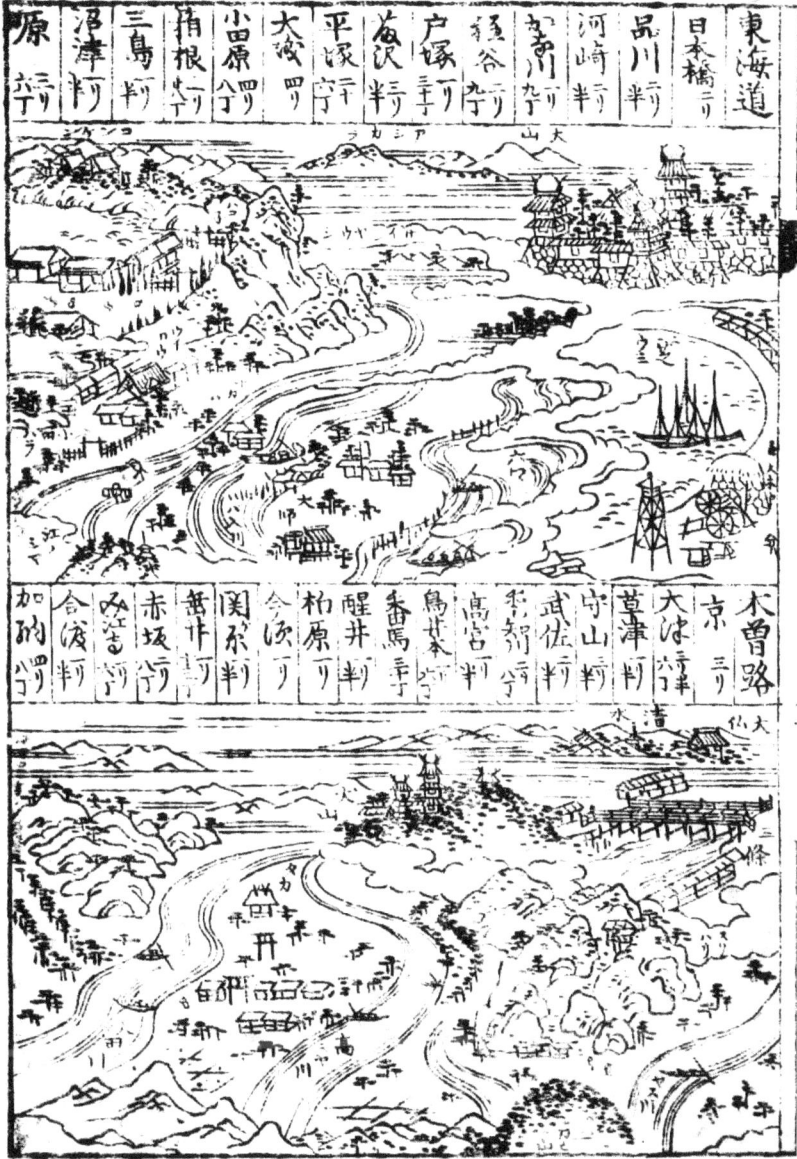

京　大　草　石　水　土　坂　関　亀　彦　吾
都　津　津　部　口　山　下　判　山　野　妻
　　ニ　三　半　半　上　半　　　判　ニ　川
　　リ　丁　　　リ　リ　リ　　　　　リ
九
行
程

合
百
北

四
里
半

十
五
丁

京

八
景
近
江

芋　板　さ　浦　大　上　桶　鴻　熊　深　本　新　倉　高　板
本　橋　い　和　宮　尾　川　巣　谷　谷　庄　町　ヶ　崎　鼻
橋　ニ　た　半　半　半　半　半　半　三　九　ニ　野　一　半
　　リ　ま　リ　リ　リ　リ　リ　リ　リ　リ　リ　半　リ　リ
　　　　　　　　　　　　　　　　　　　　　　リ
九
行
程

合
百
三

十
五
里

十
一
丁

神田明神

聖堂

平　上野

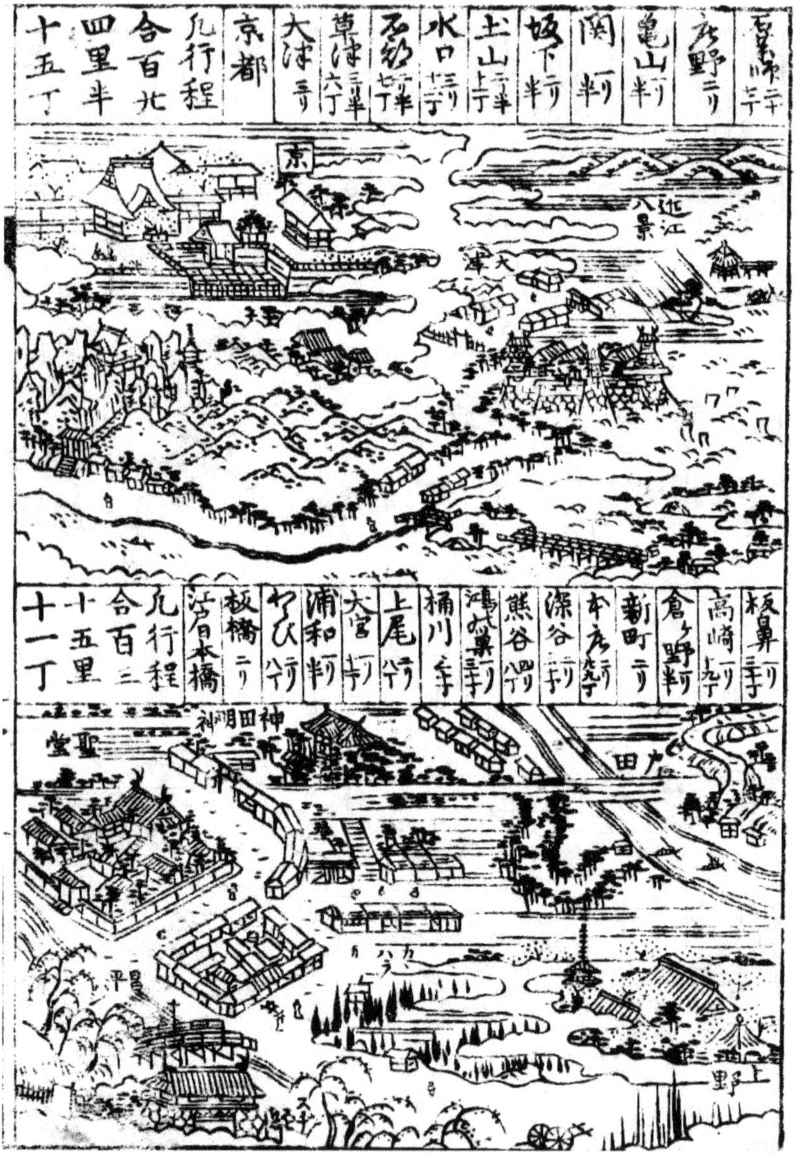

31

Tokaido from Edo to Kyoto

	日本橋	Nihonbashi	2 Ri
1.	品川	Shinagawa	2.5 Ri
2.	川崎	Kawasaki	2.5 Ri
3.	神奈川	Kanagawa	1 Ri 9 Cho
4.	保土ヶ谷	Hodogaya	2 Ri 9 Cho
5.	戸塚	Totsuka	1 Ri 30 Cho
6.	藤沢	Fujisawa	3.5 Ri
7.	平塚	Hiratsuka	26 Cho
8.	大磯	Oiso	4 Ri
9.	小田原	Odawara	4 Ri 8 Cho
10.	箱根	Hakone	3 Ri 28 Cho
11.	三島	Mishima	1.5 Ri
12.	沼津	Numazu	1.5 Ri
13.	原	Hara	3 Ri 6 Cho

14.	吉原	Yoshiwara	2 Ri 30 Cho
15.	蒲原	Kanbara	1 Ri
16.	由比	Yui	2 Ri 12 Cho
17.	興津	Okitsu	1 Ri 3 Cho
18.	江尻	Eji Ri	2 Ri 29 Cho
19.	府中	Fuchū	1.5 Ri
20.	丸子	Ma Ri ko	1 Ri 29 Cho
21.	岡部	Okabe	1 Ri 29 Cho
22.	藤枝	Fujieda	2 Ri 8 Cho
23.	島田	Shimada	1 Ri
24.	金谷	Kanaya	1 Ri 24 Cho
25.	日坂	Nissaka	1 Ri 19 Cho
26.	掛川	Kagegawa	2 Ri 16 Cho
27.	袋井	Fukuroi	1.5 Ri
28.	見附	Mitsuke	4 Ri 7 Cho

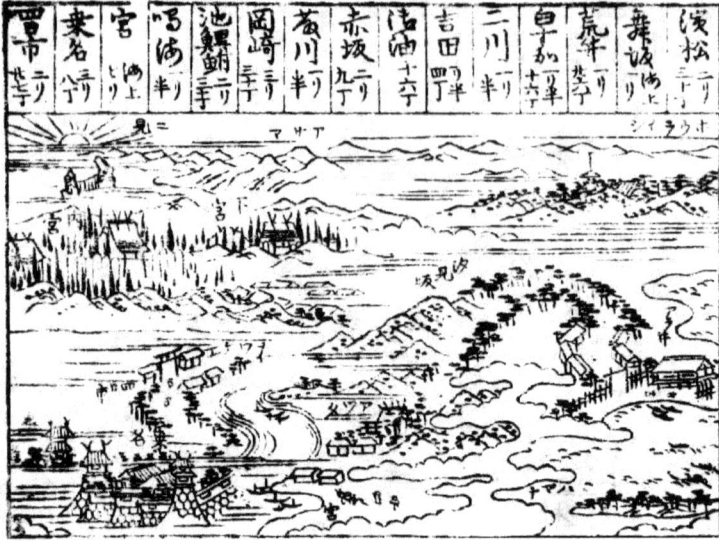

29.	浜松	Hamamatsu	2 Ri 30 Cho
30.	舞阪	Maisaka	1 Ri
31.	新居	Arai	1 Ri 24 Cho
32.	白須賀	Shirasuka	2 Ri 16 Cho
33.	二川	Futagawa	1 Ri 20 Cho
34.	吉田	Yoshida	2 Ri 22 Cho
35.	御油	Goyu	16 Cho
36.	赤坂	Akasaka	2 Ri 9 Cho
37.	藤川	Fujikawa	1 Ri 25 Cho
38.	岡崎	Okazaki	3 Ri 30 Cho
39.	池鯉鮒	Chiryu	2 Ri 30 Cho
40.	鳴海	Narumi	1.5 Ri
41.	宮	Miya	7 Ri
42.	桑名	Kuwana	3 Ri 8 Cho
43.	四日市	Yokkaichi	2 Ri 27 Cho

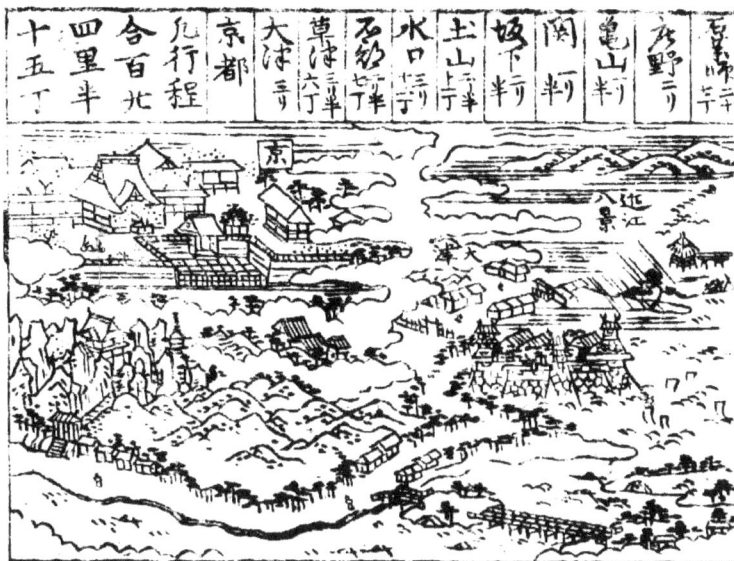

44.	石薬師	Ishiyakushi	27 Cho
45.	庄野	Shōno	2 Ri
46.	亀山	Kameyama	1.5 Ri
47.	関	Seki	1 Ri 24 Cho
48.	坂下	Sakanoshita	2.5 Ri
49.	土山	Tsuchiyama	2 Ri 25 Cho
50.	水口	Minakuchi	3 Ri 12 Cho
51.	石部	Ishibe	2 Ri 25 Cho
52.	草津	Kusatsu	3 Ri 24 Cho
53.	大津	Ōtsu	3 Ri
	京都	Kyoto	

Total distance of about 124.5 Ri 15 Cho

		Kisoji from Kyoto to Edo	
	京都	Kyoto	3 Ri
1.	大津	Ōtsu	3 Ri 24 Cho
2.	草津	Kusatsu	1 Ri 18 Cho
3.	守山	Moriyama	3 Ri 18 Cho
4.	武佐	Musa	2 Ri 18 Cho
5.	愛知川	Echigawa	2 Ri
6.	高宮	Takamiya	1 Ri 18 Cho
7.	鳥居本	Toriimoto	1 Ri 1 Cho
8.	番場	Banba	1 Ri
9.	醒ヶ井	Samegai	1 Ri 18 Cho
10.	柏原	Kashiwabara	1 Ri
11.	今須	Imasu	1 Ri
12.	関ヶ原	Sekigahara	1 Ri 14 Cho
13.	垂井	Tarui	1 Ri 12 Cho
14.	赤坂	Akasaka	2 Ri 8 Cho
15.	河渡	Godo	1 Ri 18 Cho
16.	加納	Kanō	4 Ri 10 Cho

17.	鵜沼	Unuma	2 Ri
18.	太田	Ōta	2 Ri
19.	伏見	Fushimi	1 Ri
20.	御嵩	Mitake	3 Ri
21.	細久手	Hosokute	1 Ri 18 Cho
22.	大湫	Ōkute	3 Ri 18 Cho
23.	大井	Ōi	2 Ri 18 Cho
24.	中津川	Nakatsugawa	1 Ri
25.	落合	Ochiai	1 Ri 5 Cho
26.	馬籠	Magome	2 Ri
27.	妻籠	Tsumago	1 Ri 15 Cho
28.	三留野	Midono	2 Ri 21 Cho
29.	野尻	Nojiri	1 Ri 30 Cho
30.	須原	Suhara	3 Ri 9 Cho
31.	上松	Agematsu	2 Ri 14 Cho
32.	福島	Fukushima	1 Ri 28 Cho
33.	宮ノ越	Miyanokoshi	1 Ri 33 Cho
34.	藪原	Yabuhara	1 Ri 13 Cho
35.	奈良井	Narai	1 Ri 31 Cho

36.	贄川	Niekawa	2 Ri
37.	本山	Motoyama	30 Cho
38.	洗馬	Seba	1 Ri 30 Cho
39.	塩尻	Otai	2 Ri 33 Cho
40.	下諏訪	Shimosuwa	5 Ri 18 Cho
41.	和田	Wada	2 Ri
42.	長久保	Nagakubo	1 Ri 16 Cho
43.	芦田	Ashida	1 Ri 8 Cho
44.	望月	Mochizuki	32 Cho
45.	八幡	Yawata	27 Cho
46.	塩名田	Shionada	1 Ri 11 Cho
47.	岩村田	Iwamurada	1 Ri 7 Cho
48.	小田井	Otai	1 Ri 10 Cho
49.	追分	Oiwake	1 Ri 3 Cho
50.	沓掛	Kutsukake	1 Ri 5 Cho
51.	軽井沢	Karuisawa	2 Ri 34 Cho
52.	坂本	Sakamoto	2 Ri 15 Cho
53.	松井田	Matsuida	2 Ri 16 Cho
54.	安中	Annaka	30 Cho

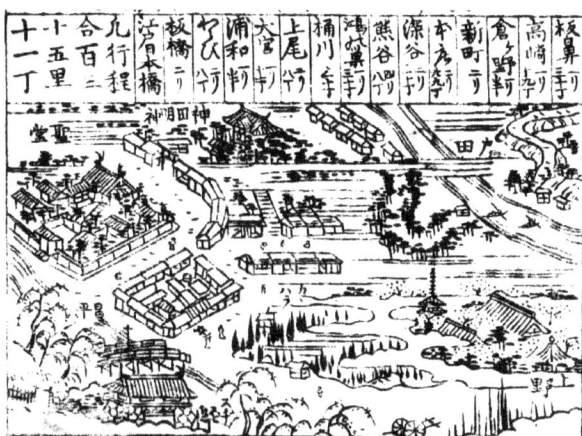

55.	板鼻	Itahana	1 Ri 30 Cho
56.	高崎	Takasaki	1 Ri 19 Cho
57.	倉賀野	Kuragano	1 Ri 18 Cho
58.	新 Cho	Shinmachi	2 Ri
59.	本庄	Honjo	2 Ri 25 Cho
60.	深谷	Fukaya	2 Ri 27 Cho
61.	熊谷	Kumagai	4 Ri 6 Cho
62.	鴻巣	Konosu	1 Ri 30 Cho
63.	桶川	Okegawa	34 Cho
64.	上尾	Ageo	2 Ri
65.	大宮	Omiya	1 Ri 10 Cho
66.	浦和	Urawa	1 Ri 14 Cho
67.	蕨	Warabi	2 Ri 10 Cho
68.	板橋	Itabashi	2 Ri 18 Cho
	日本橋	Nihonbashi	
Total distance of about 135 Ri 11 Cho			

Translator's Note: The Tokaido and Kisoji Roads

There were five major routes connecting Edo and Kyoto to each other areas. This book contains a 4 part map of two roads that connected Edo to Kyoto. The southerly Tokaido "Eastern Route" had a total length of 614 kilometers with 53 postal stations. The Kisoji, Kiso Trail, also called the Central Mountain Route was 534 kilometers long and had 68 postal stations. The Shuku, or postal stations had accommodation and other options such as boat, horse and porter hire.

The name of each station is listed with the Edo Era unit of measurements Ri or Cho.

- One Ri written as 「リ」 is 3.927km or 2.44 miles.
- And one Cho is written as 「丁」 109.09 m 357.9 feet.

五街道 Gokaidō
The Five Routes across Japan

A. Ōshū Kaidō…….. 27 Stations
B. Nikkō Kaidō……. 21 Station
C. Kōshū Kaidō……. 44 Stations,
D. Nakasendō…….. 68 Stations
E. Tōkaidō…………. 53 Stations

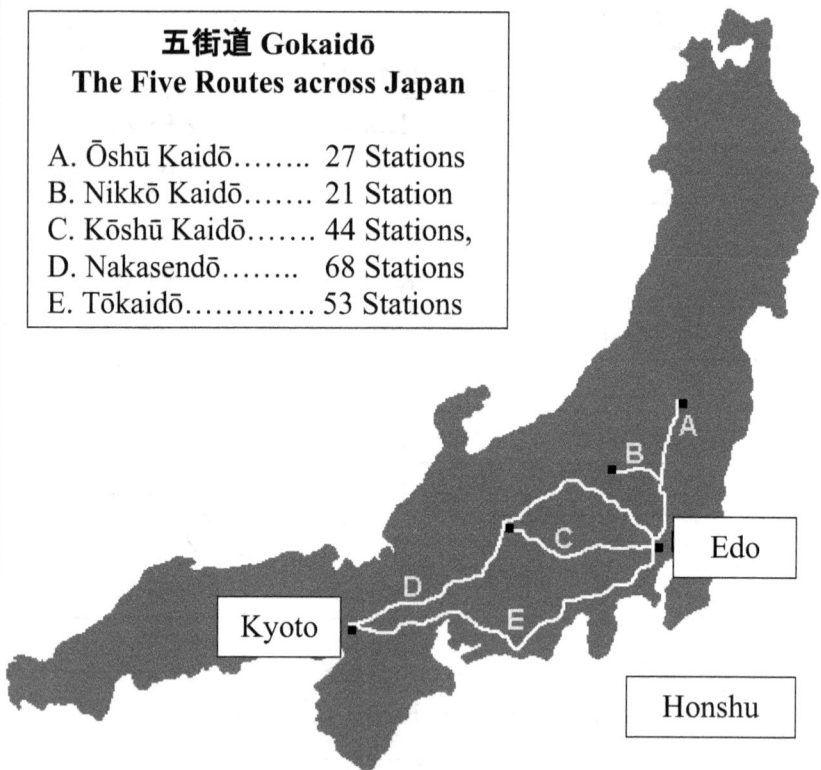

A

B

Edo

C

D

Kyoto

E

Honshu

五嶽眞形圖

東岳　泰山
西岳　華山
中岳　嵩山
北岳　恒山
南岳　衡山

抱朴子云凡修道之士樓
隱山谷須得五嶽真形圖
佩之則魑魅精怪莫能近
之昔漢武元年七夕西王
母降於承華之殿進蟠桃
命仙女董雙成許飛瓊等
奏雲璈度歌曲而為武帝
壽又以錦囊書卷示之則
此圖也故知五嶽為萬地
之宗守其形天真則世人渡
江航海隨身帶之可抑風
濤之儉亦居淨處香花供
養必降禎祥歷有奇驗可
不敬哉

陳四

ゴリ
五岳ヲタン
トハイハ書ノ
舜典ニ始リ
和漢コレヲ
酋守信スルコ
ト

ヒサシ世人
山坂河海ヲ
ワタル此圖
ヲ帶シ風
波ノ儉難ヲ
ヌ且壽福ヲ
ケル本文
アルコ
ニテシルベキ
ナリ

Translator's Note:

An Introduction to 五岳真形図 *Gogaku Shingyo Zu*
The True Illustration of the Five Sacred Mountains

The illustration on the previous page depicts the Five Sacred Mountains on top with a description of the origins of the illustrations and their powers written in Kanbun, Chinese style text below.

Revering images of the Five Sacred Mountains is a Daoist tradition from China that later came to Japan. The Five Sacred Mountains refer to specific mountains in China, each represents one of the cardinal directions and one as the center. The five images were usually printed in red and carried when traveling. This talisman is very powerful since it protects against disaster while also granting long life and prosperity.

Each image of the five sacred mountains is not a Kanji rather a drawing that captures a sense of the supernatural power of each mountain. The mountains each possess a particular supernatural power.

In Japan, veneration of the Five Sacred Mountains is part of *Sangaku Shinko,* or the religion venerating mountain gods. Sangaku Shinko is practiced all over Japan, with the biggest group associated with the worship of Mt. Fuji. Many types of people followed Sangaku Shinko and traveled through the mountains as a kind of Shugyo, intense physical and spiritual training. They carried a talisman of the Representation of the Five Sacred Mountains, in order to avoid misfortune, due to the miraculous properties.

Some of the people doing Shugyo were seeking to become Sennin, enlightened mountain ascetics. However, during their austere mountain training they need protection not only from both physical dangers like poisonous insects, wild beasts and the weather but also supernatural dangers like Yokai, ghosts and goblins.

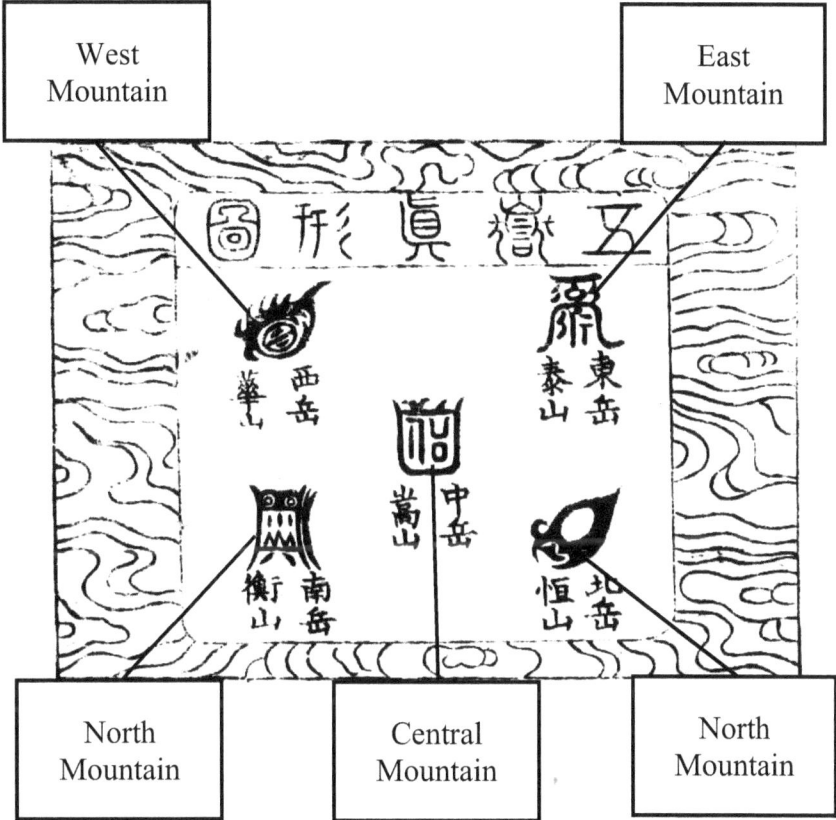

West Mountain

East Mountain

North Mountain

Central Mountain

North Mountain

	West Mountain 西岳華山 *Seigaku Kazan* Known as Mount Hua in China. Carrying this image will bring wealth and prosperity.
	East Mountain 東岳泰山 *Tohgaku Taizan* Known as Mount Tai in China. Carrying this image will prevent illness and bring long life.
	South Mountain 南岳衡山 *Nangaku Kohzan* Known as Mount Heng in China. Carrying this image will protect you from rain, lightning and typhoons. Its protections extends to supernatural enemies including devils, Yokai and overturning the effect of unfavorable constellations and celestial events like comets.
	North Mountain 北岳恒山 *Hokugaku Kohzan* Known as Mount Heng in China (same pronunciation as Nangaku.) You will gain protection of the dragon god and will therefore be safe while crossing rivers, streams and oceans, all of which are ruled by the dragon god.
	Central Mountain 中岳嵩山 *Chugaku Suzan* Known as Mount Tai in China. Carrying this image will prevent illness and protect you from disaster as it brings you good fortune. Protection from the wrath or divine punishment of Jigami, the god of the earth

五岳真形図 *Gogaku Shingyo Zu*
The True Illustration of the Five Sacred Mountains

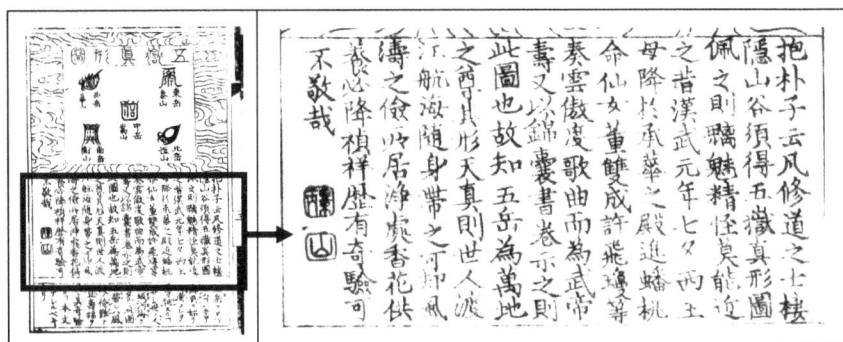

The book *Baopuzi* 抱朴子 written by Ge Hong 葛洪 (283-343 AD) says the *Illustrations of the Five Sacred Mountains* will protect you when you are doing training or just living a secluded life deep in the mountains or valleys. Keeping it will shield you from all manner of *Moh-ryoh* 魍魎, spirits and goblins.

Long ago the Emperor Wu of Han (157 - 87 BC) met the Taoist goddess Queen Mother of the West, one of the most prominent female deities in early Chinese mythology. She knows the secrets of immortality. The Queen grows the Peaches of Immortality 蟠桃 in her garden, but the trees bears fruit only once every 3000 years.

Emperor Wu, who was seeking immortality, met with the Queen, but she did not allow him to eat a peach. However, she gave him a seed from the tree and instructed him in how to grow it. If he followed her teaching faithfully, Emperor Wu would have achieved immortality, however the emperor failed to follow the goddess' instructions, and he dies. A female Taoist immortal named Tososei 董双成 helped him acquire the peach seed.

The illustration is from a later book called The Brocaded Bag Book 錦嚢書. This talisman of the Five Sacred Mountains will offer protection in all 10,000 lands (everywhere) and this representation should be carried by people crossing rivers or riding on boats across the seas. This will purify your body and protect you against maleficent spirits as it wreathes you in its fragrant flowery protection. This has been used for many ages by people expecting to encounter strange things.

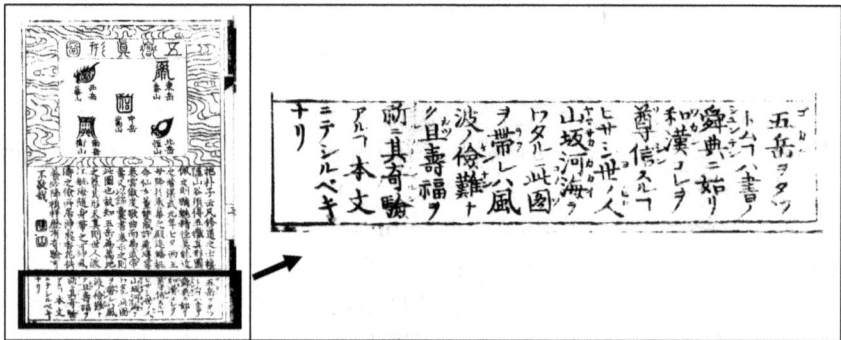

   The origins of why people venerate the Five Sacred Mountain can be found in the *Canon of Shun* chapter of the *Book of Documents,* which is attributed to Confucius (551-478 BC.) From then on the tradition continued first in China and later in Japan. By keeping a copy of the *True Illustrations of the Five Sacred Mountains* on your person you will not be plagued by wind or while on mountain roads or crossing rivers or oceans and luck will bless your journey.

How to Travel Safely in Japan
61 Cautions When on the Road

旅行用心集

道中用心六十一ヶ条

一 初て旅立の日ハ己を別而静ニ踏立て草鞋の加
減出來能試其二三日ハ間を取て度々休己を
弘痛ぬやう小きべし出立の當坐ハ人に心え
志まなく心めそび休めせず足々踏立るものなり
己を痛ますぞ獨の辛労なふなるてとまり兎角
そじめい己を大切す成し肝要とす
一 芝斗而捨もべき物懐中物其外娘む事かて
至し而教多られぞ失念物おゝく郗而頬

Ryoko Yojin Shu
Considerations for Your Journey
or
How to Travel Safely in Japan
By Yasumi Roan

道中用心六十一ヶ条
61 Cautions When on the Road

1. On the first day of your trip walk carefully in order to make sure your Waraji, straw sandals, are sufficiently broken in. For the first two or three days you should regularly to rest and to check the condition of your feet and whether they hurt or not. Everyone is excited when they first set out and are not interested in stopping for a rest, rather first-time travelers walk full of vim and vigor. However, if you overdo it and hurt your feet, it will cause no end of trouble throughout your journey. Thus it is imperative you pay attention to your feet in the initial stages of the journey.

2. When setting out on a journey you will of course carry things in your breast pocket, but overall you should limit the number of items you take. If you have too many things you will invariably loose some of them or they will become troublesome to keep track of.

3. The first thing you should do after arriving at your accommodation is orient yourself. Ask around and confirm the cardinal directions East, West, South and North. After that take a good look at how the inn is laid out, where the front and rear entrances are and where the lavatory is located. This is an old rule of thumb. This knowledge will be invaluable in case of a fire, a thief or a fight break at the inn.

4. If you are traveling for the first time and require the use of horses, palanquin or porters, you should put in a request to the proprietor of the inn the night before. Trying to negotiate directly with horse handlers or palanquin bearers will likely result in trouble along the way.

   If you are using a Dachin Cho, Official Expense Logbook, hand it over to the proprietor when you make your request. This should be done as soon as you arrive. In the evening of the day you arrive, inform the proprietor the time you wish to depart the following day. Make sure to wake up and be ready to depart by that time. If the proprietor of the inn is not awake, then awaken him. While breakfast is being made you should continue your preparations, even going as far as tying on your Waraji, straw sandals. After that you can eat your morning meal.

   If you don't get yourself fully prepared you will not be able to effectively manage the loading of horses and giving of instructions to the porters. In short, things will not go smoothly. No matter your position or class, this is something that should be taken to heart while on the road. Failing to do so will result in your preparations for departure becoming stressful.

Palanquin Bearers
From *Fifty Three Stations of the Tokaido* 東海道五十三次
By Utagawa Hiroshige (1797-1858) 歌川広重

Palanquin Bearers
From *Fifty Three Stations of the Tokaido* 東海道五十三次
By Utagawa Hiroshige (1797-1858) 歌川広重

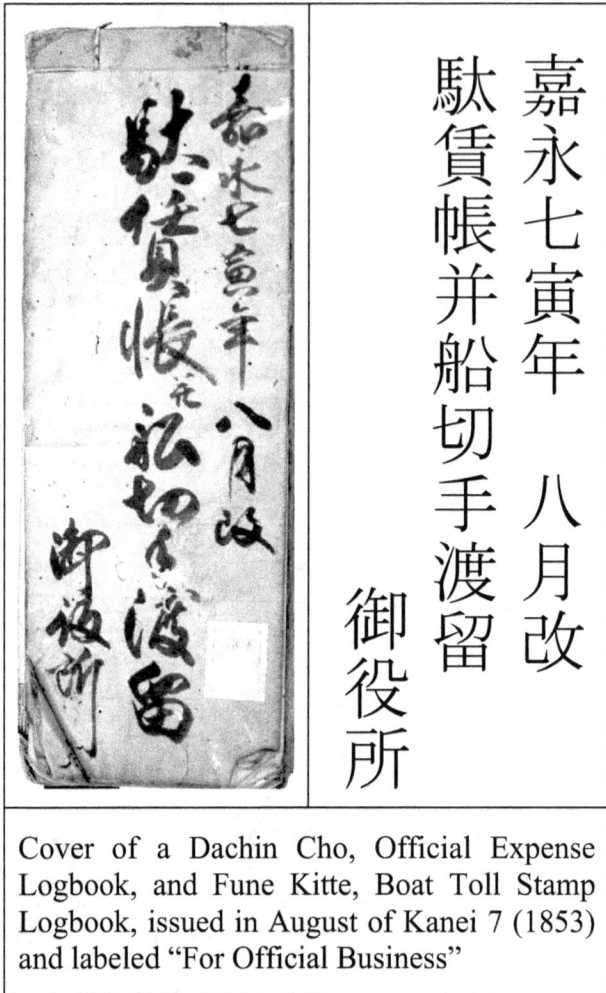

嘉永七寅年　八月改

駄賃帳并船切手渡留

御役所

Cover of a Dachin Cho, Official Expense
Logbook, and Fune Kitte, Boat Toll Stamp
Logbook, issued in August of Kanei 7 (1853)
and labeled "For Official Business"

Translation of one page of the Offical Expense Logbook, which describes its use.

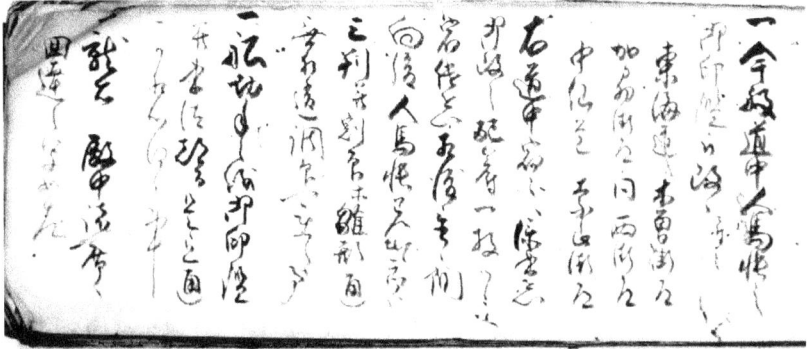

一今般道中人馬帳之
御印鑑被改候ニ付之
東海道　木曽街道
加州街道　同西街道
中仙道　奈良街道
右道中宿々へ添書を以
御改之配着一枚ヅツ
宿継を以相渡置候間
向後人馬帳差出候節
ハ三判并割印等雛形
通無相違調印可在之
候事
一船切手之儀御印鑑
并書法都而是迄通可
相心得候事
一就者殿中諸席へ
回達之写如左

This is for hiring porters or horses while on the road. An official seal is required and it is valid on the Tokaido, Kisokaido, Kashukaido, Nishikaido, Nakasendo and Narakaido.

If the bearer of this book takes accommodation at a postal station along one of the above mentioned roads, One page should be added for accommodation.

Later when this book is presented for inspection the official seals will be matched up for the use of porters or horses. This also serves as a basic travel permit.

For purchase of a toll-stamp for crossing by boat, there should be an official seal along with a description of the route.

Example of an entry from the same book

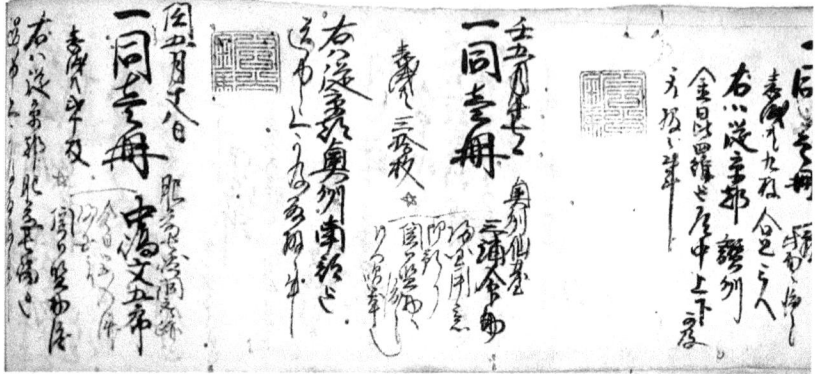

One Book
The details the transaction.

  Including the cover this book has 9 pages. The person who presented it was traveling from Kyoto to Kinbira and hired three porters for the round trip.
(official seal)

同 壱冊
此面々渡し候
表紙共九枚　人足三人
右ハ従京都讃州　金毘羅迄
道中上下可及　取扱候事
角印

5. In order to get a fresh start in the morning and not be troubled by things left behind, organize yourself the night before. Take a good look at all your items and pack your bags instead of leaving things scattered about until the day of departure. In fact, it wouldn't be a bad idea to put your Tabi socks on before going to bed. Failing to prepare yourself in such a way will result in a late start to the day. A late start in the morning will have a chain reaction and affect your whole day.

6. If you are new to an area and are staying in a Teishuku, official government accommodation, then select a place that is well constructed and seems lively, with people coming and going. Though this may cost a bit more, it will be worth it in the end.

7. During your journey you will have to endure both heat and cold. You need to be particularly careful in the summer. Your stomach might start to give you trouble when it is hot outside and you may have trouble digesting food. Therefore, when traveling, avoid eating large amounts of unfamiliar fish, poultry, shellfish, bamboo shoots, mushrooms, gourds, melons, Mochi (pounded rice cakes,) Sekihan (rice with red beans) and so on. In the summer you have to be careful not only food poisoning but also sun poisoning. These can cause a lot of suffering. Transfer your experiences from summer into how you approach eating in fall, winter and spring.

From a distance
I see the remains of snow on mountain peaks,
Yet as the days of travel compound and I draw near,
I find the slope of the mountain covered with flowers.

By Fujiwara no Kiyosuke 藤原清輔　(1104—1177)

8. Just because you are thinking, "I'm so hungry!" doesn't mean you should eat a large meal, especially when traveling. In particular eating too fast is bad. What you should do is take your time when having a meal. If you are extremely hungry, your heart is also tired. If you then eat too much, you will start to feel ill and may become sick. This is an important lesson to remember.[4]

9. You should not drink Sake on an empty stomach. Sake should only be drunk after you eat. In addition, whether summer or winter, drink Sake that has been heated.

10. When traveling you shouldn't carelessly drink Shochu. The reason is travelers often encounter bad batches of Shochu that end up being poisonous. If it is a high quality Shochu, then partaking of a little is fine. On the other hand, if you happen to be traveling in rainy summer weather or traversing land that has been soaked with rain, it best to drink a little Shochu or Awamori to rid your body of wetness. However you shouldn't drink it in fall or winter.

4

Travelers enjoying a meal at a roadside shop.
From: *The Famous Tororo Soup! Mariko Station on the Tokaido*
鞠子東海道五十三次名物とろろ汁 Hokusai

11. It is best not to get into the Furo on an empty stomach (this could refer to either an Onsen/hot springs or artificially heated bath.) Eat first, then wait an appropriate interval before going to the bath. However, if there are a great number of people at the inn, you may have to go without eating or you will end up being troublesome to other guests. If that is the case then take precautions by wetting your feet with hot water before entering the bath. Do not stay in the bath for a long period of time. It is imperative that you remember getting to the bath on an empty stomach can cause you to faint.

競細腰雪柳風呂 A "Narrowest Waist" Competition at the Setsuyanagi Bath. Artist and date unknown. Late Edo

Surprised owner of the bathhouse	Image of a mountain ascetic named Kume Sennin losing his transcendental powers and falling from the sky after seeing a woman washing her legs	Baby crying in a bucket

12. If you are staying at an inn with other guests, you will no doubt be given instructions regarding what order you should use the bath. You should always use the bath in the order you are assigned. This is because confusing the order at a busy inn can lead to friction with the other guests. If there does seem to be an error, take a good look at the other guest. If they seem to be of higher status than you, then let them go first. When traveling it is important to remember you need to deal with situations calmly. Looking at things objectively will save you in the long run.

13. If you end up completely exhausted after a day of traveling, then take a longer bath than usual. This will help you to recover. However, once in the bath do not repeatedly splash water on your face. Frequently rubbing hot water on your face will make you faint.

14. If you are on a typical journey and are not pressed for time then you should not walk at night. No matter how far you are traveling keep this rule in mind. If you are embarking on a 9 day trip, allot 10 days for the journey. This is a much better plan than trying to rush and walk at night. Further, when crossing a river and the facilities or condition of the river are not to your liking, consider the situation carefully before deciding what to do.

Text on the top right: *Pretending like the Yuban, the person in charge of keeping the water hot, is not even there. His job is to maintain the level of water and the heat in the bath.*

The guardian of the bath keeps the bath from growing cold, but it is his own interpretation.

From *Ukiyo Furo* 浮世風呂 "Bath in the Floating World"

Shikitei Sanba 式亭三馬 (1776-1822)

15. When traveling it is best to keep your sexual urges under control. Prostitutes carry diseases and in the summer heat it is easier to get infected. In addition, you can contract a skin disease from futons to its best to carry a sachet of fragrance on your person.

16. In the summer your throat will frequently go dry. However, always select clean water to drink. Even if you find an old pond or spring, if the water isn't flowing do not drink it. Such water will always have a dreadful effect on you. Carry a supply of the Chinese medicine Go-rei-san on hand to add to the water you drink. In addition, keep a supply of Sansho, Japanese pepper, as well as Kosho, black pepper. This medicine will help you to recover from bad air in the mountains as well as humidity. More details are in the back section on medicine.

Terminology Related to Prostitution in Japan:	
	夜鷹 Yotaka "Night Hawk" Ostensibly selling noodles at a roadside stall.
	女郎 Joro Works in the Yoshiwara red light district of Edo. *From : Song of the Workers of Edo* 江戸職人歌合 By : Ishihara Masaakira 石原正明 (1760-1821)
	湯女 Yuna **"Bath Girl"** Offers sexual services as part of non-sexual bath "assistance." 好色訓蒙図彙 吉田半兵衛 1686

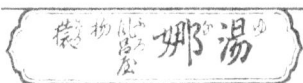

Poisonous Insects and Reptiles

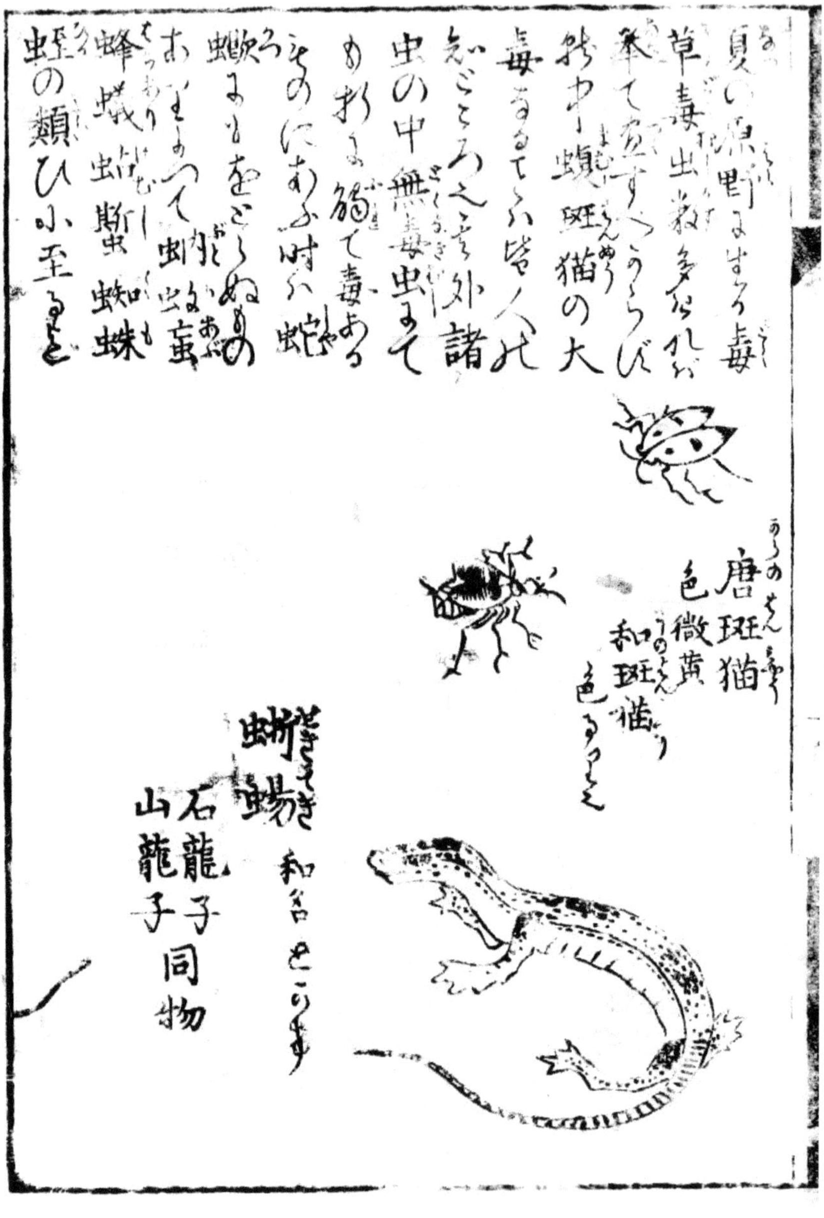

見の類を以する毒

草毒出殺多れ此

案て毒すくうらび

鈴中～蝥斑猫の大

毒するてハ皆ハ代

むさくん之を外諸

虫の中無異出すそ

の折る殖て毒ある

蜥蜴りをさらぬめ

そのにあふ時ハ蛇

おまかつて蚰蜒

蜂蛾蛇斯虫

蛾斯蛛

蚯の類ひ小至るを

唐斑猫
色微黄
和斑猫
色あるを

蝘蜒
石龍子
山龍子
同物
和名とかけ

Poisonous Snakes

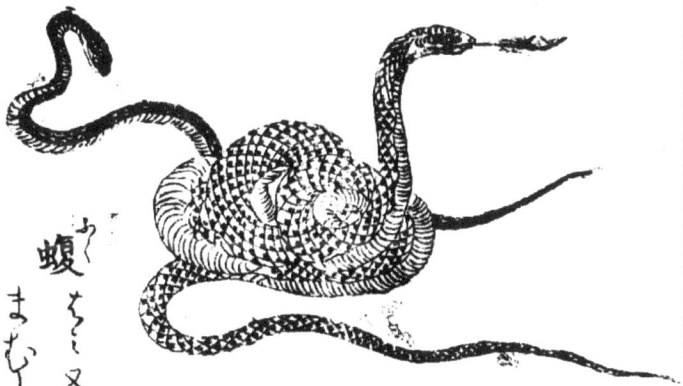

新なるべきことあり

濕熱の地を暑濕

別而甚しく毒草

異虫も多き所旅

人は恐れて山野に

体むどもとほのん

毒虫あることあり

妙業なくあるべきことあり

はあるべきことあり

その不まあり

蝮をいふ又反鼻蛇

まむし

色黒黄なり種類多

大毒あつて

烏蛇

In the summer there are a multitude of poisonous plants and insects that inhabit grassy fields. There are in fact so many that is not possible for me to record them all here. Everyone is aware of how deadly poisonous the Mamushi and Japanese tiger beetle are (Note: snakes and other small reptiles were considered "insects" at this time.) However, there are others you should take note of, such as insects that are not normally poisonous becoming poisonous in a certain time of year. That poison is easily as strong as a scorpion or a snake.

Therefore, you should avoid:
Buyo – Black flies
Ka – Mosquitoes
Abu – Horseflys
Hachi – Bees and wasps
Ari – Ants
Kumo – Spiders
Kemusi – Caterpillars
Hiru – Leech

Chinese Tiger Beetle Light yellow in color

Japanese Tiger Beetle Bluish in color

Lizards are called Sekiteki in Chinese and Tokage in Japanese. They are also known as Rock-child lizards and Mountain-child lizards.

Warmer areas of Japan can have a level of heat and humidity quite startling to the uninitiated and there are many poisonous grasses and curious insects and reptiles. I would entreat exhausted travelers to take care when resting in grassy fields or on the side of the trail in the mountains. If you are stung by a poisonous insect, refer to the medical section at the end of this book.

These are Mamushi, Japanese pit vipers. They are also called Fuku-hami, stomach biters, or Han-bi Ja, reversed nose snakes. They are typically black and yellow. There are many varieties of this snake and all are extremely poisonous.

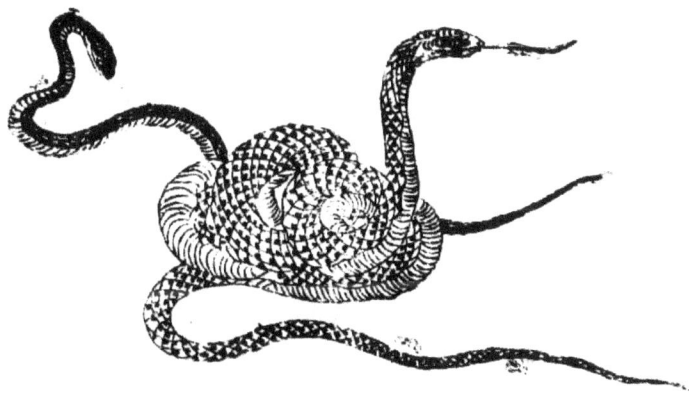

Japanese black rat snake
Note: Referred to as a "crow snake" in Japanese

17. In the summer you may see travelers overcome with exhaustion, taking a break by the side of the road or in fields. Some of these people may even be sound asleep, however you should never do that. Fields of summer grass are full of poisonous insects. Even if the insect itself is not poisonous, it may have been in contact with something poisonous and when it stings you, it can transfer that poison to your body.

    In addition, using old temples, shrines, overgrown groves of trees or caves on the sides of mountains as rest spots without thoroughly investigating them will almost certainly lead to trouble. In addition to the places listed above, take care around any spots bordering bodies of water with damp earth. The area may feel cool and refreshing, but you should not rest in such a place for long as the humidity can be the source of no end of trouble. You should stay on your guard.

18. Absolutely do not walk at a fast pace after eating a meal. This applies to when you are riding on a horse or in a palanquin. Since your food has not settled (digested) if you stumble over or fall off your horse, you could easily be knocked unconscious. Be careful regarding this matter.

19. Never mount a horse or get into a palanquin when you need to use the rest room. If you were to fall from your horse the shock on your heart would be too great and you would die.

20. If you are sending a subordinate ahead to ready your accommodation, new horses and porters, you need to dispatch them two or three days before your departure. If you do not you may end up catching up to them, thereby negating their benefit.

From : *Scene at Futamigarua* 二見ヶ浦詣
By Katsuyama Shuzan 勝山春山 Edo Era.
Note: There are two seats on either side of the saddle for children.

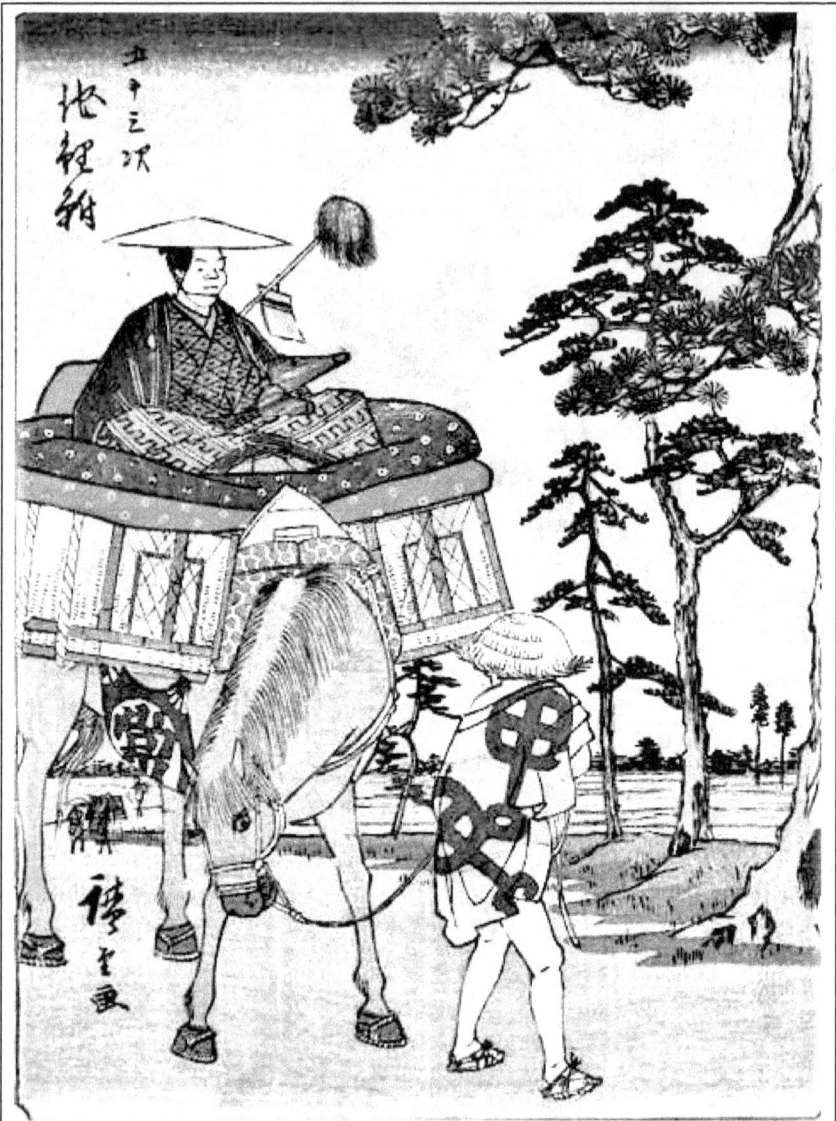

Traveling by Horse
From :*Fifty Three Stations of the Tokaido* 東海道五十三次
By Utagawa Hiroshige (1797-1858) 歌川広重
Note: Two bamboo boxes are strapped to either side of the
saddle with a large futon spread on top.

21. When you arrive at the Shukuba, postal station, you should first greet the official in charge of the station. Hand over your Dachin Cho, official expense logbook, and request the necessary number of horses and porters. After that confirm all your luggage and goods have been unloaded and inventoried. While you are doing this, take care to keep your voice low. This applies to both merchants and Samurai.

    Further, the area around the office handing such requests will be crowded so you need to be careful not to misplace anything or inadvertently cause offense to another traveler.

22. Whether you are a Samurai or an average citizen, if you have been given an important task by your lord, you need to refrain from getting into debates with horse handlers, palanquin bearers or porters. Even if things are not going as you would like, it is important to keep your temper under control. The only exception is if the actions of the men you hired are affecting the fulfilment of your task. If not then keeping yourself under control is the most important lesson.

    Getting involved in some sort of situation with your hired help may interfere with the completion of the important mission you have been charged with.

23. During your journey you will have to change horses and porters. Seasoned travelers know that this is when a lot of mischief can occur so they have to really be on guard. Ensuring items don't "wander off" during the changeover is stressful and troublesome, nevertheless it is something you must commit yourself to. Since the horse handlers will be quickly shifting your goods from one horse to another, my advice is to help out during this process. You will then be able to prevent small items like Kanzashi,[5] coins on a string, from falling out. As you are helping, use that time to keep track of all your small items.

---

[5] Kanzashi was a string threaded through the hole in small denomination coins for easy transport. Officially the Kanzashi written 銭緡 also called Zenizashi 銭緡 was a string of 1000 coins that was equivalent to 1 Kan, which is roughly $12,500 today. At one point in the Edo Era 1 Kan was actually 960 coins.

Rent Collector
Illustration from the Edo Manga *Lord Fudo of Mikawa Island Edo.* 1789. The collector is on the left with several Zenizashi over his shoulder.

24. When placing clothing or packages wrapped in paper inside your Akeni, bamboo travel case, be sure to double wrap it in oiled paper in order to prevent your items from getting wet. This is because when you are crossing river, water may splash in through the gap under the lid. This also applies to Ryogake, wicker trunks carried on poles. You should consider how to prevent water from getting inside. Overall, keep in mind that it is easy for items to get wet or lost when crossing rivers, so great care should be taken.

If you are looking for a good Akeni or Ryogake, I recommend the shop Sugawaya, located in front of Dentsu Temple in Edo. They make reliable products you can trust.[6]

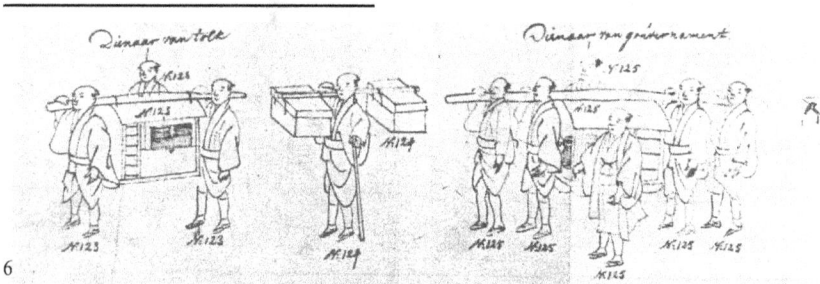

Unknown Edo Era Dutch illustration of porters. Left is a standard palanquin, center is a Ryogake and right is a high class palanquin.

A horse loaded with bamboo trunks wrapped in oiled paper.
From *Kiso Kaido: View of Asayama*
木曾街道追分夜浅間山眺望 by Ei Izumi 英泉 Edo Era.

25. If, during the course of your journey, you come across an unknown river, you should absolutely not attempt to cross it on foot. That being said, if the bridge has been washed you may have to cross a section of river on foot or by boat. Before crossing a swollen river, however, you should consult the proprietor of your inn. You should never attempt to cross on your own or direct your porters to cross. You should defer to the discretion of the proprietor of your inn or the local official. This is the best way to cross safely.[7]

---

[7] In the Edo era in order to prevent insurrection/civil war the Bakufu central government banned the construction of bridges over large rivers. This was to curtail the movements of large armies should a local warlord decide to stage a revolt.

Poling Across the River at Mitsuke
From *Fifty Three Stations of the Tokaido* 東海道五十三次
By Utagawa Hiroshige (1797-1858) 歌川広重

Approaching Mount Misaka, I see showers falling on the Cloudy Slope approach, I cross in the interval.

By Nijo Tameshige 二条為重 1325－1385

26. If you are traveling with a woman and will have to cross a river during your journey, it is best to talk to her about what will happen in advance. Women, unlike men, are nervous creatures and upon seeing the rushing waters of a wide river may become fearful. She may also be so surprised at the sight of the rough looking men that handle the river crossings that she may go into a daze.

    Therefore, in the days before you are to cross the river, make sure to talk with her to gauge how she might respond. Also ensure she understands that if separated not to panic. Typically crossings have officials on duty so there is no real need to worry, however women are timid so you should keep this advice in mind.

    This applies not only when crossing rivers but also when traveling by the shore, crossing by boat, on mountain roads and so on. The best thing to do is talk to her in advance.

27. When crossing a river or boarding a boat, be careful with the items you carry in your breast pocket. In addition when you are riding in a palanquin make sure you don't drop anything inside. An item dropped in the water will surely be difficult to recover.

28. When boarding a boat at the dock they will sometimes also be transporting horses. If so, then allow the horses to board first and people should board afterward. Horses can get irritated on boats and become violent, thereby injuring people. However if you are traveling with women or elderly people do not board a boat transporting horses.

Crossing a River by Rendai, Water Palanquin
From *Fifty Three Stations of the Tokaido* 東海道五十三次
By Utagawa Hiroshige (1797-1858) 歌川広重
Note: Rendai 蓮台 were palanquins carried by teams of four porters. Rendai is also the name of the lotus flower that serves as the seat of Buddha and Bodhisattva.

Crossing a River by Rendai, Water Palanquin, at Odawara
From *Fifty Three Stations of the Tokaido* 東海道五十三次
By Utagawa Hiroshige (1797-1858) 歌川広重

Note: The Rendai were constructed of wood with a Tatami mat seat. They were carried rather than floated across the water

Crossing a River by Kata-gurma
From *Fifty Three Stations of the Tokaido* 東海道五十三次
By Utagawa Hiroshige (1797-1858) 歌川広重

Note: Kata-guruma "shoulder-car" was a cheaper way to cross a river than using a Rendai, water palanquin.

According to the 島田市博物館 Shimada City Museum the rates for crossing depended on the depth of water. This sign indicates the prices in the Kansei Era 1789-1801. Starting on the right side: Thigh-deep $14, Below the Belt $15, Above the Belt $20, Nipple Level $23, Armpit Level $28. If the river was more than 4 Shaku 5 Sun deep (136 centimeters) crossings would stop for the day.

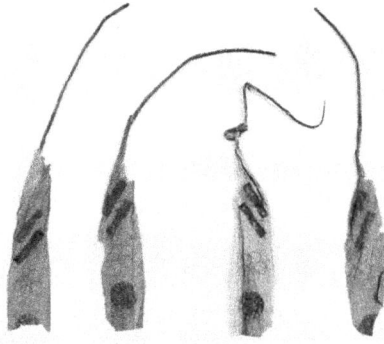

Once the price was decided for the day, travelers would buy Kawa Fuda 川札, river crossing tickets. These would be handed over to the porters who would tie them to their topknots or headbands before crossing.

29. You should consider the situation carefully before taking a boat that purports to be a shortcut. If you are on an important assignment and are in a rush, it is best to stick to the overland route. On the other hand, if you are traveling and not pressed for time, traveling by a boat and relaxing as the wind pushes you along will no doubt be a grand time. Keep in mind that if the weather were to change suddenly you might end up regretting your decision. This would be a serios situation if you were on official business. There are several other cautions regarding riding boats, but I will cover these in the chapter *Traveling by Boat*.

30. If you find yourself at a river that is swollen from rain or melted snow, it is a bad idea to walk up and down the banks looking for a place to cross. A river in such a state will be rushing by at a furious pace and innumerable objects will be swept downstream, potentially causing serious injury. In addition, you may happen upon a river near the base of a mountain. While such a river may appear to be an unremarkable shallow stream, if it is the time of year when snow begins to melt, or you are deep in the mountains and an evening rain starts to fall, understand the water in that little stream can increase rapidly and widen to a starling degree.

    This is why a permanent bridge has not been built in such a place. Locals will build a temporary bridge for use in the winter time. However, it will get washed away when the river rises. The Sakawa River on the Tokaido is one such place. Others are the Shiazawa River on the Okukaido and the Odawara River. This is a common phenomenon in mountainous areas of Japan. When the river is high, clearly you shouldn't attempt to cross on foot. However, even if you see a temporary bridge in the water absolutely do not attempt to cross. Due to the high waters the posts have been pulled free and the bridge is probably floating. People have been washed away in such cases.[8]

---

[8] This seems to contradict entry 26, "Typically crossings have officials on duty so there is no real need to worry, however women are timid and you should keep this advice in mind."

31. Following a long period of rain it is not uncommon for sections of mountains to crumble down. In such cases avoid accommodation located at the foot of mountains with a large stone slab hanging above. Also accommodation on the banks of a river should be avoided. Take a moment to consider the recent weather before proceeding with your journey.

32. If you have hired porters, palanquin bearers or horse handlers and are paying for their accommodation be sure to give each person their wage and accommodation fee each day. If you don't have a sufficient amount of small coin, then change out some money when you arrive at your accommodation, then immediately pay your workers.
    Generally speaking, you need to be cautious about borrowing or lending money while on a long journey. Even if you are recording such transactions in your diary you may find the figures do not add up at the end of your trip.

33. In the course of your long journey you may end up traveling with the same people for 3, 5 or even 6 days. Even though the other travelers may seem trustworthy, do not make arrangements to stay at the same inn, share food or exchange medicine.

34. If you find yourself without a horse to carry your luggage, some people will ask to load their goods on a fellow traveler's animal. I do not recommend doing this, even if the person is someone you know. The reason is along the way you may suddenly need something from your luggage. However, since your goods are loaded onto another person's horse you may cause them an inconvenience. No matter who you are, or what your status, when on a journey you should only rely on yourself and not ask others to help you.

35. If you are going to be traveling in a group then five or six people is the limit. More than that is not good. People don't all think alike and if you have a large group of people on a long journey you are going to have one person that doesn't get along with everyone else.

36. Here are some of the kinds of people you shouldn't travel with. People that drink a lot of Sake, people who don't drink Sake but have other particularities, temperamental people, asthmatics or people with a chronic disease. You never know when these conditions will flare up, so consider carefully before traveling with people that have those afflictions.

37. If you are carrying your travel money on your person while walking, it is best to keep most of your money in a Hara-maki, stomach-wrap style wallet. Keep just enough money for each day in a small wallet in your breast pocket. It goes without saying when refilling your wallet from your waist wrap to do it at night when no one is watching. This is very important.

Departing from Kyoto, it was still the season of green leaves on trees. However as I reached the border of White River, it had edged into autumn and the fall leaves were scatted about me.

Minamoto no Yorimasa 源頼政 (1104-1180)

38. When staying at an inn, store your Katana and Wakizashi under your bedding. Store your Yari (spear) or Naginata (halberd) at the base of the wall.

39. You should be extremely cautious about fire while on the road. This applies not only to when you are passing through villages but also when walking through fields. Never carelessly throw out a smoldering piece of tobacco. Even when taking a break or riding on a boat there have been cases of fire starting on peoples clothes or luggage. You should remain vigilant.

40. In the spring you will see farmers burning fields here and there. If the wind is strong when they are conducting burning, the fire can spread with alarming speed. When passing by a village doing this take a moment to consider were the safest path lies. Don't ever take the sight of burning fields as a joke.

41. As you walk along the road you may pass a house or field with trees loaded with Japanese pears, persimmons, yuzu, mikan or other fruits. It doesn't matter how ripe they may be do not, under any circumstances, casually pluck them. In addition, a village may have spread out harvested Gokoku, of the five grains: rice, barley, foxtail millet, soybeans or common millet. Be careful not to inadvertently step on that or any other thing the villagers have set out in their gardens to dry. When you are a visitor in an unfamiliar area, causing offense, even if unintentional will always end poorly even if you are not at fault. I recommend you keep this in mind.

42. If you are traveling in the mountains or through fields and pass by a young woman, a group of women cutting grass or a cluster of people that includes women, offering a word of greeting is appropriate, but refrain from chatting beyond that. Further, never mimic a local person's accent, way of speech or snicker at them. Quarrels and fights spring from such minor incidents.

43. There are times when you will have no choice but to stay at an Ai no Shuku, Interval Inn, or some other non-standard accommodation well-off the main road. You will no doubt be uncomfortable about this, however you should not complain when staying in such a place. The secret when spending the night in an Interval Inn is to speak in a manner quieter than usual and take special care when arranging your luggage and locking the door.[9]

44. If you are traveling to a place you have never visited or even heard about before, no doubt their way of speaking as well as their manners and customs will be different. Since they speak differently, you may have a hard time understanding the locals and making yourself understood. You will probably find many things in such an area strange but understand that without a doubt the locals also find your mannerisms and way of speech strange. With that in mind, mocking or laughing at those differences will be insulting to the people living in that area. Making a joke out of how someone speaks or making it clear you are looking down on people will lead to an argument.

45. As you are walking down the road you may hear a person singing part of a Noh play, a ballad or part of a Joruri puppet play. While you may be tempted to join in, please refrain. This can often lead to an argument.

46. While on the road it is best to not stop and loiter with crowds watching certain things. If you do happen to come across a fight, an argument, a group gambling, a game of Go, Shogi, a village dance, village Sumo wrestling, the body of a person who died in an accident, a murder scene or any other large group of onlookers, it is best just to pass without stopping. This applies to any large group of onlookers.

---

[9] The Ai no Shuku, Interval Inns, were rest stops that illegally offered overnight accommodation. They were called interval inns because they were often built between two legal establishments.

47. You may be staying in a town for an extended period that has nothing to do with selling products. For example you are in town for therapy at an Onsen, paying your respects at a temple or shrine or maybe heavy rains have caused the river to rise and therefore delay your passage. It goes without saying you should not do any sort of speculative buying of property in distress or goods from a bankrupt business. In addition, you should absolutely never gamble on games of Go or Shogi. Further, even if you see a business you are familiar with, never attempt to involve yourself with a local company of the same type and begin making deals. Your desire will be the start of a problem. At the very least you will end up with a troublesome situation and at worse you will bring disaster upon yourself. It is best to refrain from such activities.

48. The air around Onsen often has a lot of sulfur fumes in it. This will rust not only the blades of your Dai-Sho, long and short swords, but also the outer fittings. You should be careful. Though it is true that you don't have to worry about rust at some Onsen, for the most part rust will start to affect your weapons when you stay in that area. The chapter on Onsen at the end of this book will elaborate on this and contains advice.

49. If you are traveling on assignment for your lord or are on an important trip, you should avoid even the slightest deviation from your route. Do not veer off course to visit historic ruins. In addition, do not take any unknown shortcuts or board unfamiliar boats.

50. If you are staying at an inn when a fire breaks out nearby, get yourself ready quickly and then gather your important things. If you are traveling with retainers then light a Chochin, paper lantern, to lead your escape. Be sure to not leave anything behind. This is the one time you do not want to rely on the innkeeper to take care of things for you.

51. At some point during your journey you may end up sharing a room with another traveler. This is not a problem if you exercise sufficient caution. The first thing you should do is ensure the doors and windows are all properly secured. Having done that, take a moment to observe your fellow traveler. If he seems like a heavy drinker or a bit strange then immediately take whatever steps you feel are necessary. Incidents involving unknown travelers together in a room are not uncommon.

52. If the other guests at the inn you are staying at start a big drinking party that looks as if it will continue until morning, you and your other fellow travelers should take turns staying awake until it ends. During a big drinking party problems often occur so it is best for someone to stay awake until it finishes.

53. Horses are animals that easily startle. If your horse does get spooked and start racing off do not immediately jump off, instead grab hold of the packs on the back of the horse. Wait until the packs begin to slide off. Dismount only when they seem like they are going to fall to the ground. Carelessly leaping form a horse is going to lead to a big injury.

54. Take special care in March and April if you have rented a horse from someplace in the middle of nowhere. This is particularly true when mounting or dismounting. Horses owned by people living in the countryside are not used every day and are typically well rested. Since they are only worked occasionally they can go into heat in the spring and dash off. You should exercise caution when riding such an animal.

55. If your horse is stung by a horsefly it may suddenly bolt. Take special care in the summer. Also, people tend to get drowsy while riding in the summer and this can be dangerous. Exercise caution when on mountain slopes or if the route takes you alongside the bank of a river. Pay particular attention to children and elderly people when traveling on horseback in summer.

56. If you happen to be staying in the same room at an inn with another customer who tries to sell you some miracle remedy, you should firmly refuse. If you require some medicine go to an apothecary.

57. If you are serving as the supervisor of Hikyaku "Flying Legs" couriers or other porters, treat the duty seriously regardless of the status of the sender. It is important to take all such jobs seriously since documents can often be worth more than their weight in silver or gold. If you were to drop or misplace such a document the person who commissioned you will won't be able to complete their important work. Great care should be taken so their information will not slip into the hands of another person.[10]

58. Samurai must carry their Dai-sho, long and short swords, while on the road. However choose ones that are light and on the short side. Avoid carrying excessively long Katana or Wakizashi short sword, especially ones sheathed in unusual or fashionably decorated scabbards. In addition, do not wear a Kimono with an unusual pattern or carry any curious goods or bags. By avoiding carrying items that draw attention, you will also avoid disaster.

---

[10] Hikyaku 飛脚 couriers carried letters, documents, bills of exchange, and packages, using a system of relay stations that began in the 12th century until the late 1850s.

59. If you are traveling with retainers, manservants or other hired help, you should gather the whole household and all their families before you depart. Have an honest discussion about what to do if someone should fall sick and die along the way. In a worst case scenario, a person traveling with you falls ill and dies then have the hotel and a local doctor write a note to that effect. In addition, when traveling alone or when departing for a cross-country tour around all of Japan, carry a Tera-jomon with you. By being well-prepared you will avoid trouble.[11]

---

11 A Tera-jomon, also called a Kera Uke Jo, is a Temple Certification. Temple Certifications were documents carried by travelers issued by local temples certifying a person as being in good standing and "not a Christian." Possibly travelers on long journeys could be suspected of traveling for the purpose of proselytizing.
The following page contains a translation of a Temple Certification issued by 東長寺 Tochoji Temple in 1812 for a certain Kanuka Shiro Uemon.

寺請状之事 *Tera Uke Jo no Koto*
Record of Issuance of Temple Certification
From the Sōtō School of Zen Buddhism

This document covers six members of the Kanuka Family issued to Shiro Uemon. The above persons have for generations and without interruption been Zen Buddhists and maintained a family temple.

With regards to the prohibition against belief in the Christian religion. I, as a representative of this temple, stand as absolute witness to these people.

Following this investigation I hereby issue this Temple Certificate regarding the above matter.

November of 1812
Morioka Domain Tsugaruishi Zuiunji Affiliated Temple
Attended by Lord Isobe
Lord Enzan Sho Saemon

Since the snow started to fall, all the mountains have grown in height, whichever is Mt. White Root, I cannot say.

Minamoto no Morotiki 源師時 (1077-1136)

60. If there is a solar eclipse while you are walking, take a break and resume after it has passed. The same applies in the case of a lunar eclipse.

61. There's probably no need to say this in reference to temples and shrines, but never write calligraphy on bridges, columns, boulders and so on. Also absolutely do not paste a paper sticker on any of these.[12]

This ends 61 rules of traveling. The following sections contain other important cautions.

---

[12] 千社札 Senja-fuda are paper stickers that pilgrims would paste to the ceilings of a temple or shrine, or even to the pillars of a Torii gate and crossbeams of high-ceilinged shrines.

They are generally rectangular with the pilgrims name and address written on them. Initially they were hand written but later people would commission single color, usually black, woodblock prints. Around the same time the practice of pasting O-rei on temples and shrines went from a sign of religious devotion to a kind of hobby. Pasting the stickers in hard to reach places became popular and collapsible poles to fix the stickers to high ceilings were developed.

Examples of various Senja-fuda

Hachijoji Island

FEUDAL MAP OF JAPAN
BETWEEN 1573–83
Provinces in Capital letters
Daimyo in Italics
Smaller Daimyō

Exercising Caution as the Water Changes

Invariably, a few days after arriving in a new area your stomach will begin to give you trouble. This is due to the "change in water." You may have loose bowels or you may become constipated. Blisters and rashes may also appear on your body. This will be in addition to any chronic illness that may be bothering you.

Many people think, "Though I am going to another Domain in Japan, the Earth is all under the same heaven, so just as the air is the same, so will the water. There is no need to worry." Unfortunately this is not the case. Depending on the geography of that place there can be more differences than just the properties of the hot springs. There will be differences in heat and cold, the weather, the kind of people you meet and even the types of food you eat.

For example, if you were to catch a fish from a mountain stream and release it in a lake, it would appear stunned and confused for quite a while. This applies to people as well. Until you have lived in a place for one or two months, you will suffer from various ailments.

The weather in Kanto, the eastern area of Japan, differs from western areas like Osaka and Kyoto. In addition as you travel further west to Kyushu, the weather changes more. If you are going up north to the domains of Eichigo and Mutsu you will encounter entirely different weather.

Should you travel to a domain by the shore or an island, it won't just be the name and shape of the land that differs. Imagine how unfamiliar things could be. Interestingly if a person from an area with a warm climate goes to a cold area they will have trouble enduring the cold. However, if a person from a cold area goes to a warmer area, any cold weather in that area will not adversely affect them.

Long ago many people living on Hachijo Island[13], traveled 287 kilometers north to Edo for work, however due to a smallpox and measles pandemic, most of them died. This is because they weren't adjusted with that land and its weather.

---

[13] See the map on the previous page.

Therefore, I would like to conclude this chapter by cautioning anyone being sent to work in a distant domain or even someone traveling to visit an Onsen, to be careful for the first two weeks or so. This includes not only what you eat and drink but also your everyday activities. I will introduce some effective medicine to take in another chapter.

If you are on official duty then before you set off walking, hire Yuki-fumi, "snow stompers" to clear a path and guide you. However, average travelers will clearly not be hiring guides and you should be aware that you are unlikely to meet anyone on the road to ask directions. It is not uncommon for people to lose sight of the road and become lost.

Therefore, I would like to conclude this chapter by cautioning anyone being sent to work in a distant domain or even someone traveling to visit an Onsen, to be careful for the first two weeks or so. This includes not only what you eat and drink but also your everyday activities. I will introduce some effective medicine to take in another chapter.

Things to Remember When Traveling in the Cold Domains

If you are embarking on a trip to Oshu or Kitaetsu, you need to be careful of everything from breakfast onward. In cold regions snow begins to fall in September and by the time of Ebisuko[14] in October its falling everyday covering the fields all around.

In addition, up north it is usually powder snow that falls. This means even on days when there is no snowfall, wind can blow the snow about so fiercely it seems like a blizzard. On days when the snow falls, you can watch as one or two Shaku, 30 ~ 60 cm, of snow accumulates. That being said it falls so fast you can't even see the footprints of a person walking in front of you.

---

[14] The Ebisuko festival is held in northern Japan. Traders hold a festival to make offerings and pray for good business.

If you are a big drinker of Sake and are traveling in the colder domains of Japan, absolutely do not drink to excess. When you consume great quantities of Sake, your body becomes hot, and no matter what kind of blizzard there might be, it doesn't affect you. Since the fields and mountains are all covered with a blanket of snow, you cannot tell the road from pasture or rice field. As far as you can see it is all flat, so, since you are drunk, you stride off with great confidence and eventually lose your bearings. People in such a state often fall into ditches or trenches and freeze to death. It is hard to discern the road at night.

Therefore, you should eat a solid breakfast and be sure to carry a grilled rice ball for lunch in order to prevent yourself from growing hungry. If you get hungry, the cold will begin to affect you and your strength will ebb. Once you are weakened, the snow storm will blow you over.

If you are not drunk on Sake and find yourself in a snow storm it is possible to survive the night without dying. Most people who freeze to death in blizzards in the Oshu and Kitaetsu regions do so not because they have drunk a little Sake, but because they have drunk a great deal of Sake.

If you get caught in a snowstorm a member of your party may lose feeling in their hands or feet due to freezing and topple over. You should light a fire of rice straw, not right beside them but a short distance away. This will also help people who have become ill [disoriented/hypothermic] due to the cold.

In addition, if you or a member of your party have become extremely cold and you are planning to heat up using a bath, make sure the water is only lukewarm. Then gradually increase the temperature. Warming a person using extremely hot flame or extremely hot water will cause them to pass out.

Illustrations of Tools You May Need When Traveling In Cold Countries

When traveling through cold counties be sure to wear a Kamiko, a woven-paper shirt, or a Wata-iri, a Kimono that has cotton stuffed between the layers. Another option is leather underwear. It is hard to put into words how cold it gets in snowy countries and how deep the drifts of snow can get.[15]

Shoes and woven rice grass footwear suitable for areas that get a lot of snow should be purchased locally. It may be possible to obtain them before you set out, however in certain areas you may not be able to use them.

15

A Kamiko paper shirt on display at the *Paper Museum in Tokyo.*

(No text.)

The *Natetsugi*, Avalanches, in Cold Countries

When walking through Ohshu or Echigo you will encounter stretches of trail with tall mountains shooting up on either side. These sections can be 2 ~ 3 Ri or even 4 ~ 5 Ri[16] in length. In late February, around the time of Higan, equinoctial week when Buddhist services are held, spring starts to affect the great mounds of snow. The snow on the mountains on both sides of the train begins to melt. Then, when strong east winds blow, or thunder rumbles, or an earthquake strikes or the branches of trees rub together the snow begins to crumble and fall into the valley. This phenomenon, when accumulated snow on the mountains on either side of a valley fall in a rush all at once, is known colloquially as *Natesuki*, avalanche.

It is not uncommon for a person walking along the trail when this happens to be buried under the *Nate*. In most cases this results in sudden death and there is no way to prevent it.

In addition, when a person is reported buried by an avalanche the people do not immediately begin digging them out. It would be impossible to find them, so the only recourse is to wait until the summer heat has melted the snow enough for them to recover the body.

---

[16] One *Ri* 里 is 3.927 kilometers or 2.44 miles.

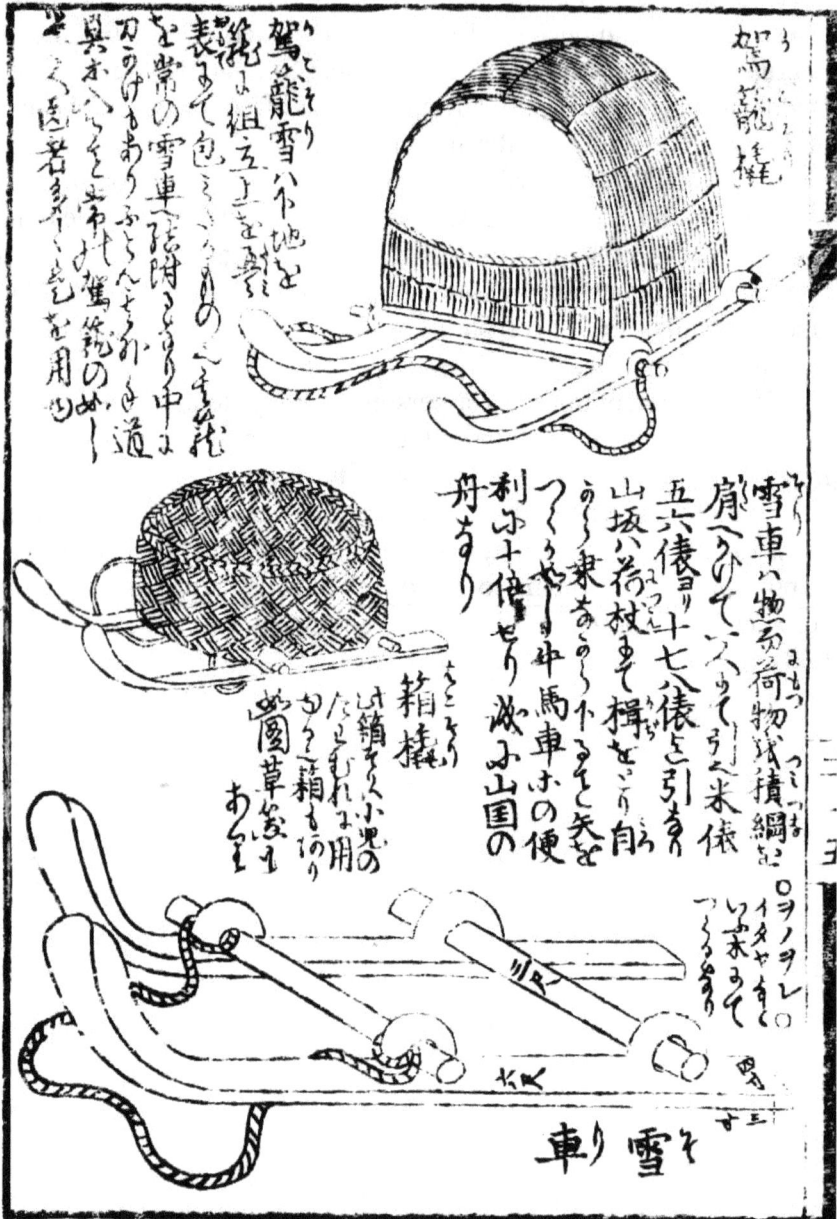

ろ
駕籠橇

とをり
駕籠雪ハ下地を
綱を組立上を貼
表そて包さくろ
裏きて包さくろもの
刀こもありふしんそくり道
具ふへくを常し駕籠のやう
く医者等さいを用り

雪車ハ物而荷物或積綱を
扇へふそくへ引之米俵
五六俵より十七八俵さ引き
山坂ハ荷杖まて掉を
のく東あうく下をと矢を
つくへやり中馬車小の便
利小十倍セり凌小山国の
舟すり

さころ
箱橇
け箱さくし児の
たるされば用
竹の箱もさり

さころ
常草笠も
ある王

○ヲノヲレ○
イタヤそく
い久ろそ
つくる子り
つくる子り

四寸
五寸

そり雪車

Common Items found in Cold-Weather Countries

Protective Clothing Worn in Cold-Weather Countries

Clothing and Footwear Worn in Cold-Weather Countries

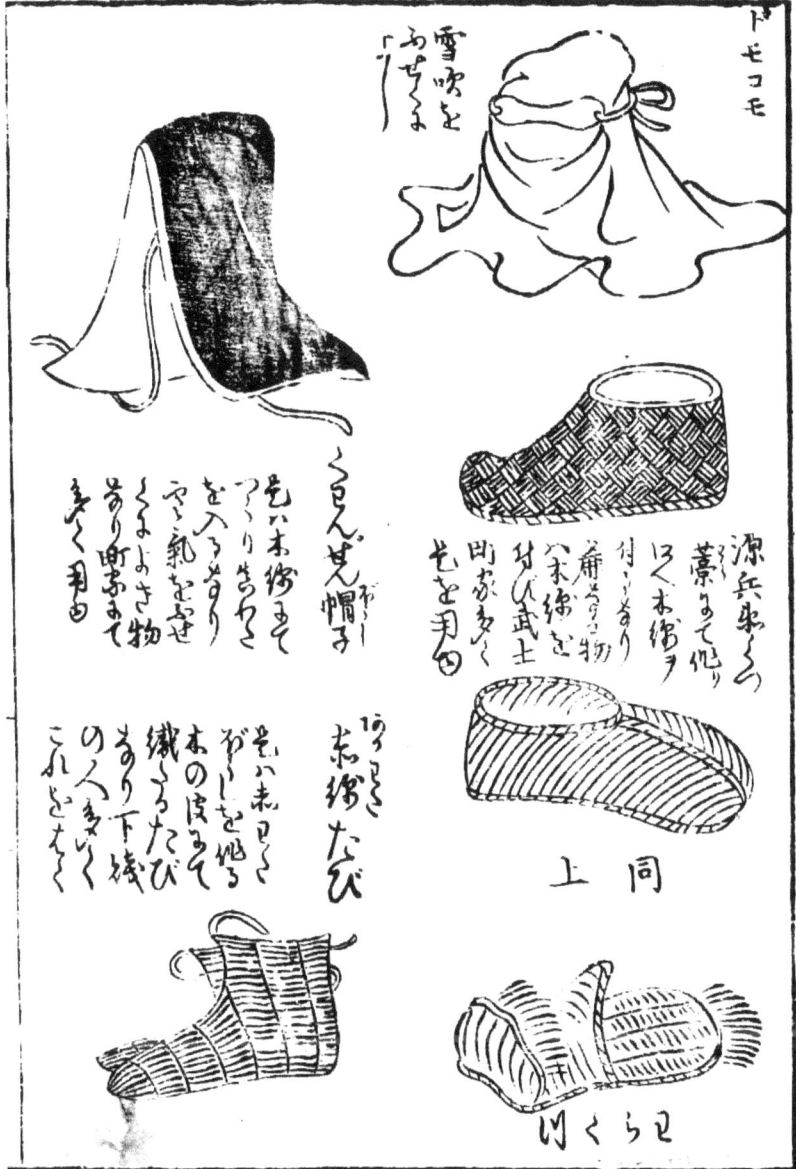

Snow and Ice Footwear Worn in Cold-Weather Countries

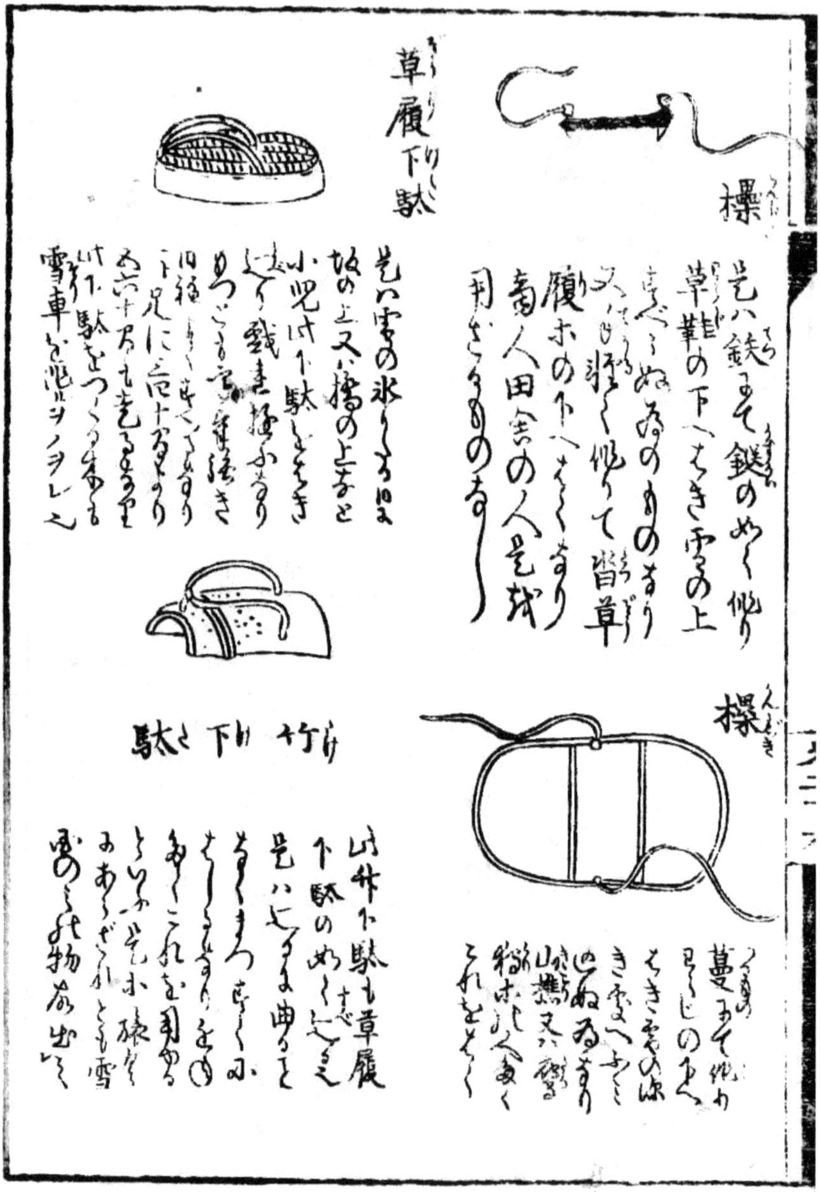

草履下駄

標

駄と下り竹け

標

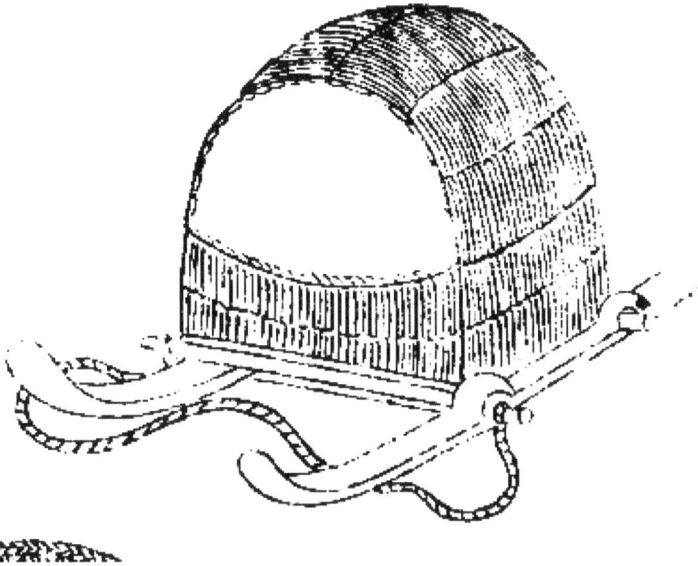

Kago Zori Palanquin Sled

The frame of a palanquin-sled is made of bamboo, then it is covered with the same woven bamboo grass mat that are used on Tatami mats. Next, the whole thing is attached to a regular pair of skis. Inside the palanquin-sled a futon is spread out and there is even room for small tools. Since there is also a Katana-gake, sword rack, it seems like a regular palanquin. People of high status and doctors frequently use these.

These sleds, called Sori, or snow carts in Japanese, are typically loaded with goods and pulled by a passing a rope over your shoulder. Typically, 5 or 6 bales of rice can be pulled on a sled, but 7 or 8 bales is not unheard of. When going down slopes you can ride on the backs of the skis and use a pole to steer. Riders fly like an arrow down slopes. Palanquin-sleds can be used to pull ten times the amount a horse or cow could. You could consider the sled to be "the boat" of snow countries.

Hako Zori Box Sled

The Box Sled is a toy that children play with. The top is not always a wooden box, sometimes, as shown in the illustration, a woven grass basket is used.

Boards from Azusa (Japanese cherry birch) or Kaede (maple) trees felled by axes are used to make skis. The bottom board is 6 Shaku (180 centimeters) long and the cross pole is 3 Shaku (90 centimeters) long.

150 cm

15 cm

12 cm

24 cm

18 cm

Kosuki Snow Paddles

Kosuki are made of wood from the Buna, Japanese beech, tree. There are also ones with longer handles of 8 or 9 Shaku (240 ~ 270 cm.) These wooden paddles are used to scrape snow off the roof of your house. After the snow has been scraped off, locals use the snow paddles to cut the snow and stack it up like a wall of stone blocks. In some places the walls are stacked so high you can't see over them but there is a path to walk between.

These paddles are also used to clear the roads after a big snow and even carried as walking sticks when going down snowy roads. Children also use snow paddles as a plaything and carry one while walking about until the snow melts.

	### *Yuki Fumi* Snow Stompers The snow stomper is made of Wara, woven rice straw. Locals will step inside one of these with both feet and use it to stomp the snow down. After a snowfall this tool is used to pack down the snow in front of their houses. They also use it to pack the road down and make it passable. Occasionally empty rice bales are used for the same purpose.
	This is another sort of snow stomper used in the same way as the one above. This tool is typically used after the basket type snow stomper, in order to further compact the snow. It is made of slats of thinly split Buddhist pine wood. This seems like an essential item but not every house has one.

	Kabuto Zukin Helmet Hood Also called a Chohan Kashira. Made of leather and cloth.
	Wara Kasa Woven Rice Straw Hat
	Wara Gutsu Woven Rice Straw Shoes These are like Tsune-ate the shin-guards on Samurai armor. They are very common in the Echigo area.
	Akawata Boshi Red Cotton Hat Made from the bark of trees.
	Wara Habaki Woven Rice Straw Pants You can find Kama Habaki, made out of woven cattail stalks but the ones made out of woven rice straw offer better protection against the cold.

	***Tsuma-saki Waraji* Tips of the Toes Shoes** Also known as Orifuki Waraji and Kokake Waraji.
	***Domokomo* "No Matter the Weather"** These are very useful in protecting yourself in a snowstorm.
	***Genpei Gutsu* Genpei Shoes** These are made of Wara, woven rice straw, with cotton stuffed into the opening. Cruder versions have no cotton inside. You often see Samurai and townspeople wearing these.
	Same as above.
	***Wara Gutsu* Woven Grass Straw Shoes**

111

	***Kanzen Boshi* Full-cover hat** This is made of cotton with rough cotton stuffed between the layers. Offers excellent protection against the cold. Many city-dwellers wear these.
	***Akawata Tabi* Red Cotton Split-toed Shoes** Also referred to as Red Cotton. They are made from the same tree bark as the Akawata Boshi hats. You often see lower-class people wearing these.

Kanjiki Crampons

These are made of iron and resemble Kasugai, large staples used in carpentry to hold two pieces of wood together. This is tied on below the sandals or shoes in order to prevent slipping on hard-packed snow. Kanjiki crampons are simple to make and can be tied onto the bottoms of an kind of shoe. Traders in the city and country folks all use these.

	***Kanjiki* Crampons (Snowshoes)** These are made from woven vines and tied underneath shoes. They help to prevent you from sinking into the snow. They are frequently used by lumberjacks and people going hunting with hawks.

Zori Geta Platform Shoes

On days when the snow is frozen hard, kids will put these on and slide down hills. They also slide down from the peaks of bridges. When winter is in full swing, kids can really slide a long way. With one push they slide 30 or 40 Ken. These are made with the same wood that was chopped down with axes and used for skis.[17]

Ta-ke Geta Bamboo Platform Shoes

These are another type of shoes for sliding on ice and snow, similar to the ones above. Bamboo Platform shoes allow you to slide straight without turning. These have become quite fashionable of late. Bamboo Platform shoes are not something you will need while traveling , however since they are only found in snow countries I thought I would introduce them here.

---

17 One Ken 間 is 1.82 meters.

There are some people that have to travel to snow countries in the northern parts of Japan, by command of their lord or official business. If you do have to travel in this area, be sure to check the temperature for the past few days as well as what the climate is like this time of year for the region you will be traveling. After arriving, ask the locals as well.

Stay aware as you walk along, taking particular care not to develop a cough. I encourage you to ask the local people for advice, as they will help you out.

Be aware there is the danger of encountering an avalanche on the roads connecting Joshu, Aitsu and Echigo. Along the way you will see stone memorials to the people that died from Natetsugi, avalanches

How to Avoid Crossing Paths With Wild Animals Whilst on Mountain Trails

When walking deep in the mountains, or across wide plains, travelers should try to talk amongst themselves or with other people that happen to be journeying down the same trail. This is because bears and wolves will hide when they hear human voices.

People traveling alone do not talk so if an animal is sleeping beside the road, it has no warning they will encounter a human. This means they get startled and therefore bite.

There isn't any danger of this happening in the middle of the day however, encounters such as those described above happen when traveling at night. Therefore, when walking alone in the mountains, countryside or any other place where people are few and far between, carry a bamboo walking stick with the bottom end split. By splitting the bottom of the bamboo walking stick you will make noise as you move down the trail. You can also use a walking stick with a stone attached to the bottom. By doing so, wild animals will hear you and run off. Also, when traveling by night, if you carry a Hinawa, fuses, or Taimatsu, torches, you won't encounter wild animals.

Hinawa is the slow burning fuse used to light matchlock guns / arquebus. They can be made out of cotton or bamboo fibers.

Palanquin bearers carrying Taimatsu torches as they climb Mt. Hakone at night. 夜中松明とり From 53 *Stations of the Tokaido* 隷書東海道五十三 by Utagawa Hiroshige 歌川広重.

Other Advice For Traveling in the Mountains

- If you smear the bottom of your Waraji straw sandals with cow dung before you begin walking down a mountain road, snakes, particularly Mamushi, Japanese pit vipers, will retreat before you. It will also scare off poisonous bugs.

- By carrying a Talisman of the Gogaku or Hakutaku in your breast pocket you will be able to avoid disaster. These talisman will also prevent wild beasts and devils from molesting you.

Dealing With Magic

If you suddenly lose track of where you are, it may be because a Tanuki, racoon dog, or Kitsune, fox, has cast a spell on you. Other common tricks they play are to cause the area around you to suddenly become dark, make a river appear where none should be, manifest a locked gate where no gate should be and so on. The best way to handle these situations is to first try and calm down. Sit and smoke some tobacco and try to think back on the route you took to get here. If that doesn't work then walk back down the trail to the last crossing and look for a house. Explain your situation and ask for advice. By doing this you will be able to shake off any trickery Tanuki or Kitsune have cast on you.

Taking a moment to relax and evaluate your situation is good advice, not only when traveling but all aspects of your work and family life.

Four Pieces of Advice For When Traveling By Boat

- As soon as you board a boat take note of all the tools you see, as well as the location of poles and trapdoors. If you are caught in a squall and the wind and rain cause the boat to flip over, you can use the boards and poles to keep you afloat. Observing what is in the boat can prevent people who cannot swim from drowning.

- When out on the ocean a large sea creature may begin bashing into your boat. If that happens, don't panic, instead crouch in the shadow of the bottom of the boat and grab a piece of wood or something. Start banging it on the deck and the sound will cause the creature to leave.

- The sea is a wild place. A Tatsumaki, or waterspout, could erupt beside your boat, or black clouds appear over the sea, causing the seas to start boiling and a great whirlpool to form. While the captain of your boat is no doubt experienced, you should nevertheless toss a board or piece of woven grass mat into the maelstrom. This will cause the whirlpool to momentarily calm and give your boat a chance to escape.

- Crowding onto a boat is never a good idea. First of all, being on a boat with that many people is going to be uncomfortable. In addition, it will make it hard for the rowers to work. On another note, you should always follow the instructions of the captain. His decisions are final and you should never try to enter a debate with him. There is a rhyme and reason for everything that goes on aboard a boat, and causing trouble can result in the boat developing a hatred of you. The most important thing you can do is stay out of the captain's way.[18]

---

[18] The last entry contains two different pieces of advice. The passage implies it is the boat itself that will develop a hatred of you.

Seven Helpful Ways to Avoid Seasickness

1. If you have become seasick and have thrown up everything in your stomach, your throat will no doubt be raw and parched. What you need to do is drink a child's urine. If you can't obtain any then urine from an adult will suffice. Accidentally drinking water in this case will result in sudden death. Take great care.

2. Drinking a mouthful of the water from the river before you get on a boat will prevent you from becoming seasick.

3. Before boarding a boat collect a pinch of earth from the ground near the bank. Fold it up inside a piece of paper and secure it under your belt so it is against your navel. This will keep you from getting seasick.

4. A pinch of sulfur folded inside a piece of paper and placed in your breast pocket will prevent sea sickness.

5. Also if you inconspicuously slip 2 or 3 Tsuke-gi, matches, into your breast pocket, you won't get seasick.[19]

6. In addition, drinking a mouthful of strong vinegar is good. Chewing on an Ume-boshi, dried salted plum, is also an option. Drinking the juice from a fresh Daikon radish is helpful.

7. If you are violently vomiting and cannot get it under control, mix equal parts of Hange, Chinpi and Bukuryo in a pot and stew it.[20]

---

[19] Tsuke-gi are long thin strips of wood with the tips dipped in sulfur. Japanese style matches.

[20] *Hange* 半夏 Crow-dipper used to treat upset stomachs.

Chinpi 陳皮 Sun-dried tangerine peel helps with digestion.

Bukuryo 茯苓 A subterranean fungus that resembles a small coconut. Helps relaxation.

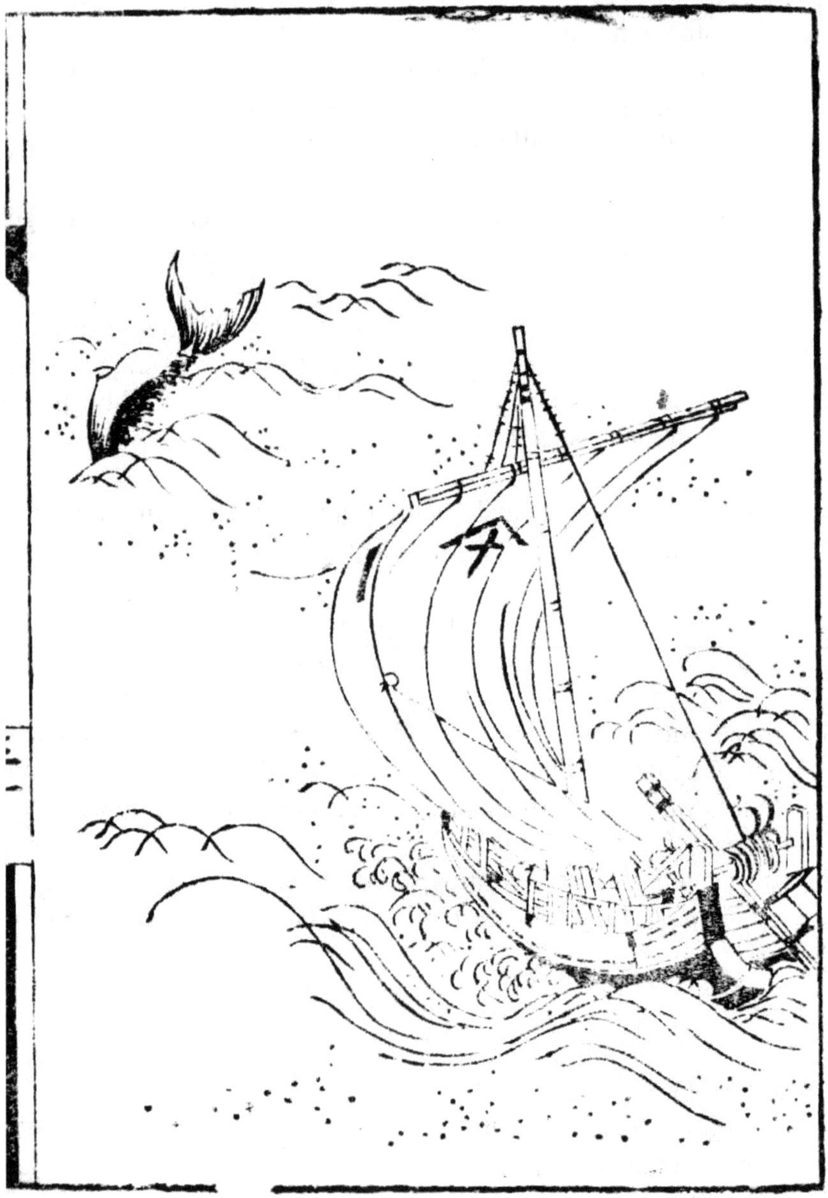

(no text)

Three Ways to Avoid Motion Sickness in a Palanquin

1. If you are prone to motion sickness, ride with the door of the palanquin open.

2. If you take a stalk of Nanten[21] or "heavenly bamboo" and place it upright in the center of the palanquin you are riding in and focus on it, you won't get motion sickness. If a traveler has become ill, add some ginger extract to hot water, mix it thoroughly and drink. Absolutely do not give an afflicted person cold water.

3. If a woman is going to ride on a horse or in a palanquin, tie a thin belt securely around the point known as Mizu Ochi, the solar plexus, before beginning your journey.

---

[21] Nanten "heavenly bamboo" is actually an evergreen shrub

First Aid For When You Fall Off a Horse[22]

If you feel ill after falling off a horse and there is blood in your saliva it is best to mix powdered Renkon, lotus root, with Sake and drink it. Also you can mix powdered Hasu no Ha, lotus leaves with sake and drink it.

In addition, if you landed on your backside, hip or leg and blood has flown to that area, forming a bruise, then you should immediately go to a surgeon and have him bleed you. If you do this, the wound will heal faster.

Remember that sweat from horses is quite poisonous, ensure you don't get any in your eyes or in your food.

22

A painting of the priest Hensho falling off his horse whilst gazing at flowers

僧正遍昭落馬図 by Hanabusa Iccho 英 一蝶 1652 ~1724

How to keep poisonous insects away

Carrying a pouch filled with a strong smelling substance is the best solution.

It's a good idea to carry a mix of powdered dried ginger mixed with powdered Orpiment, a volcanic mineral. If those are not available you should be able to make a sachet of "dragon's brains" the borenal plant "camphor brains" camphor wood and musk.[23]

How to keep fleas away while on the road

If you spread cuttings of fresh Sophora directly on your futon it will keep fleas away. This grass is found all over mountains and fields and if you pay attention you can collect some as you travel. Just crumple the plant up and spread it on your futon. Sophora is shown in the illustration on the following page. Look at the illustration carefully and remember it.

---

[23] Musk is a substance with a persistent odor, obtained from the caudal glands of the male musk deer.

Illustration of Kujin, Called Sophora in English

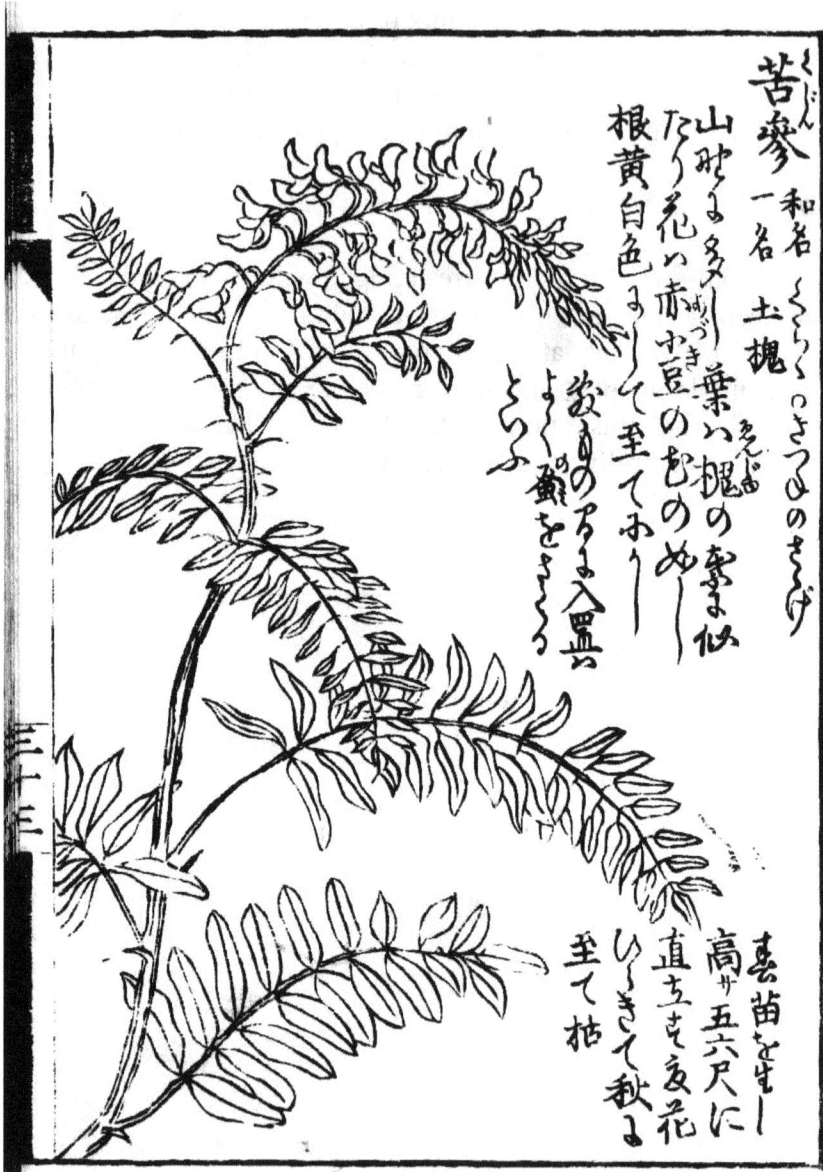

Sophora
Kujin is the Chinese Reading
Its Japanese name is
Kurara but it is
commonly known as
Fox's Gift or the
Japanese pagoda tree.

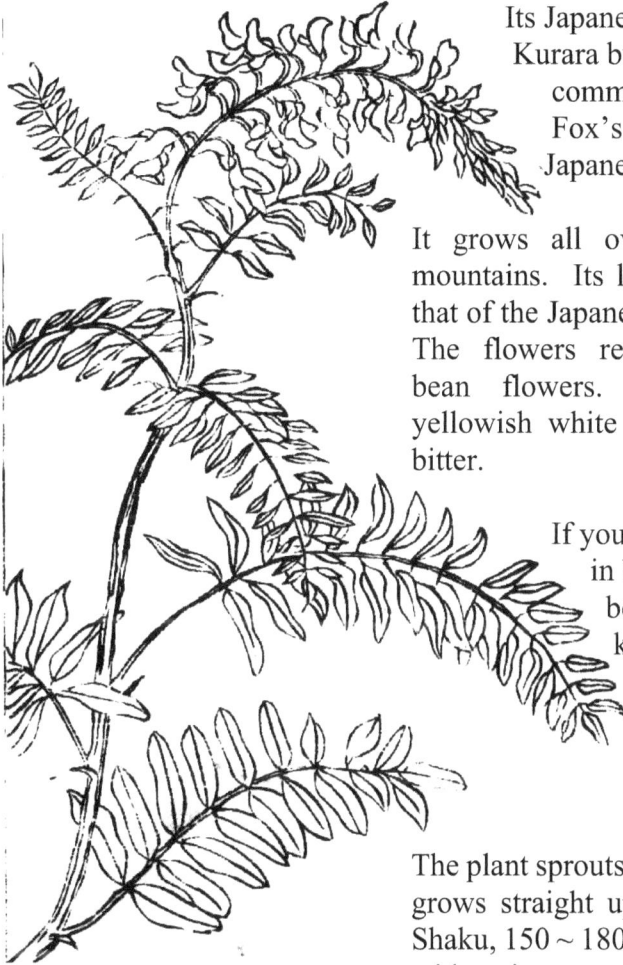

It grows all over fields and mountains. Its leaves resemble that of the Japanese pagoda tree. The flowers resemble adzuki bean flowers. The root is yellowish white and extremely bitter.

If you place the plant
in between your
bedding it will
keep fleas away.

The plant sprouts in spring and it grows straight up about 5 or 6 Shaku, 150 ~ 180 centimeters. It withers in autumn.

125

- If you hold on to the fruit of the Japanese bitter orange tree while you sleep, fleas will not bother you.

- You can also dry knotweed and spread it out on the floor under your bed.

- Boil down a large number of Japanese bitter oranges and then soak your underwear in it. If you put them on after drying them thoroughly, the dyed material will repel fleas.

Secret and unusual methods to recover from exhaustion on the road

- When you take a break at a tea house do not just sit on the raised porch with your legs hanging off the side and your Zori sandals still tied on. Even if you only have time for a short break be sure to take your Zori off, and find yourself a good position to relax in on the porch. This simple act will quite mysteriously refresh you.

- New travelers who get exhausted or find themselves with blisters on their feet should realize that the problem is their Zori sandals are not tied appropriately. You should make sure you make or buy proper Zori, and that they are broken in until they are comfortable. Never rush when tying your Zori and they should be neither too tight nor too loose. If your feet are dry you are carrying too much heat, which causes them to hurt and leads to blisters forming. Therefore you should untie your Zori from time to time and allow the heat to dissipate. When doing this be sure to make yourself comfortable.

- If your feet are exhausted and starting to hurt, go into the bath as soon as you get to your accommodation. After that rub salt into the bottom of your feet and roast them in front of a fire. This will be mysteriously effective.

- If you find yourself completely worn out after you take a bath, spray Shochu on your legs from the point called Sanrin down to the bottom of your foot. If you rub the Shochu in instead of spraying it on your legs, it will not be effective. [24]

- If, after walking for a long time, you find the arch of your foot is severely swollen and painful, find a worm, and, with the earth still on it, grind it into a paste. Rub this on the bottom of your foot.

- If you are exhausted do acupuncture on the following three points: Sanri, Shozan and Tsukoku. See the illustration on the following page for these points.

- If you develop blisters on the bottom of your feet, mix powdered Hange, or Pinellia tuber, with a few grains of cooked rice and rub it into your feet.

- Along those lines, you can take the stub of a cigarette and knead it with a few grains of cooked rice. After rubbing it into your foot, roast the area before a fire.

- Additionally, if there is a pharmacy nearby, see if you can buy the medicine known as Chinese Soil, or white lead. Mixing it gently with a few grains of cooked rice and applying it to the area will be effective.

- Also, for a blister, first thread a needle with cotton thread. Then brush ink onto the thread using ink from your Yadate, portable brush and ink writing set. Pierce the blister from one side and out the other. This will force the water out and leave the ink behind. Quite mysteriously this will cause the pain to stop.

- Dissolving some of the flour used to make Udon noodles in water and rubbing it on the affected area is also effective.

- When traveling in summer the bottom of your feet may become hot and painful. Applying the green juice that results from grinding up leaves of the knotweed plant will be effective.

---

[24] Sanrin is detailed on the following page.

Illustration of Acupuncture Points on the Leg

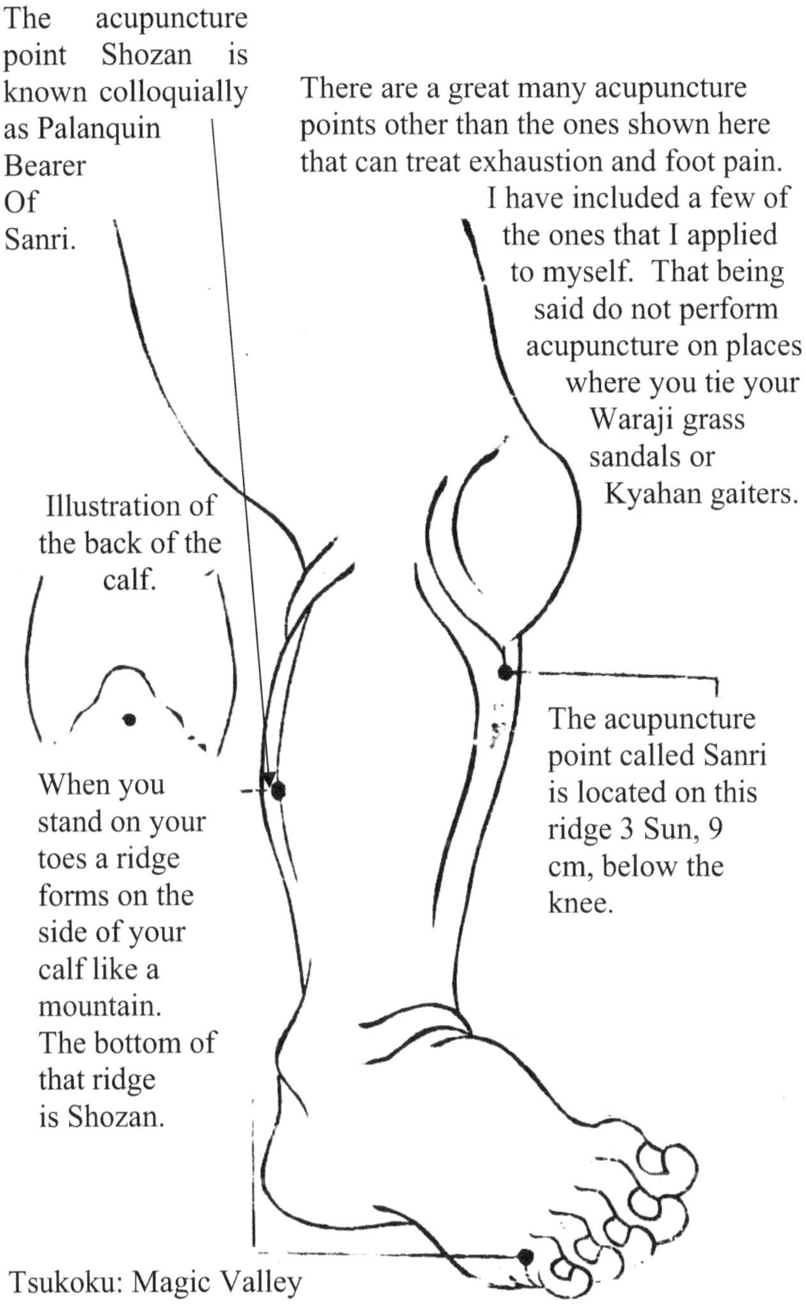

The acupuncture point Shozan is known colloquially as Palanquin Bearer Of Sanri.

There are a great many acupuncture points other than the ones shown here that can treat exhaustion and foot pain. I have included a few of the ones that I applied to myself. That being said do not perform acupuncture on places where you tie your Waraji grass sandals or Kyahan gaiters.

Illustration of the back of the calf.

When you stand on your toes a ridge forms on the side of your calf like a mountain. The bottom of that ridge is Shozan.

The acupuncture point called Sanri is located on this ridge 3 Sun, 9 cm, below the knee.

Tsukoku: Magic Valley
This refers to the depression on the side of the little toe. If you do acupuncture on this point, you will be able to recover from exhaustion.

- When traveling in summer, hang some leaves from the peach tree from your straw hat. This will, quite mysteriously, dissipate the heat.
- If you swallow one or two grains of pepper every morning you will not get heat stroke. In winter it will help you to avoid blizzards.
- When drinking water in summer, chew up and swallow a grain of pepper. Swallowing the crunched up grain of pepper with water will prevent you from getting ill from bad water.
- If you are stung by a poisonous insect the best thing to buy some Enreitan cream or Sokoen cream and rub it on the spot. The pain will disappear just like that.[25]
- Stew pond snails in soy sauce and then dry them. Carry a supply of them while on the road and eat them for two or three days after you arrive at your destination and you won't suffer from indigestion due to water poisoning. (water poisoning refers to water you are not used to drinking)
- How to treat a person who has stayed in the bath too long
- If stays in the bath too long and begins to get light headed spray their face with cold water. If their bloody nose doesn't stop, and they continue to be dizzy, splash their entire body with water.
- In addition, after spraying their face with water, comb all the knots out of their hair. Combing their hair continuously to free all the tangles will, quite mysteriously, enable them to recover. Giving them a bit of vinegar to drink will also help.

Medicines that are good to take when traveling

- **Kumanoi** Dried Bear's Gall Bladder
- **Kiyogan** Mysteriously Effective Pills[26]

---

[25] These are brand names for multi-purpose ointments.

[26] Kiyogan, Hankontan, Goreisan and Kosho are all brand names of prepared medicines.

Advertisement showing the shop that sells two prepared medicines called "Kan and Riui"
Edo Era
By Utagawa Kunihisa 歌川国久 画 (1832-1891)

- **Hankontan** Reanimating Pills
  These all help with cramps and other stomach pains as well as food poisoning and heat stroke. There are other stomach medicines, but these three will serve you well.
- **Goreisan & Kosho**
- When you enter a new area and the water changes, these medicines will help. In addition when you are traveling in summer, mix this with the water you drink when you are thirsty.
- Sano-toh Powdered Stew of Three Yellow Herbs
- You can become nervous when traveling which can lead to constipation. This is the best time to take out this medicine and use it.
- Kirimogusa cuttings of mugwort used in moxibustion treatments Be sure to carry it so it doesn't get wet while traveling.
- Bikyuen Sudden Need Pills When you come down with food poisoning and even when you throw up you can't find relief. That being said, try this after you have taken Kumanoi Dried Bear's Gall Bladder, Kiyogan Mysteriously Effective Pills or Hankontan Reanimating Pills and found they made you throw up.
- Abura-Gusuri, Oil Medicine, an external medicine made of fat mixed with various medicines.
- Hakuryuko White Dragon Ointment: a brand of ointment for cuts.
- Baikako Cherry Blossom Fragrance: Oil made from cherry blossoms mixed with various medicines. Used for the hair and scalp.

In addition to these the medicine Keikako has recently become available from the Asakawa region. Keikako or Flowery Incense from the Judas Tree is made from the bark of the camphor tree. It is used to treat cuts, swelling and insect bites.

This ends the section on medicine you should bring with you on a trip. Each person should bring the medicines that they feel work the best for them. Sticking to what you know is best. When you are on the road, have a pharmacist make your medicines. Even if you are struck suddenly with a major ailment, they will be able to help you.

What You Should Bring on a Trip

Yatate, portable brush and ink case
Senseu, folding fan
Itohari, needle and thread
Kachukagami, pocket mirror
Nikitecho, diary and record book (one volume)
Kushi, a brush

And finally, Bintsuke Abura, oil to arrange the hair above your ears and behind your temples. This spot is known as Bin.

Note that you can borrow a razor from the inns along the way and use that. Also you should bring along pieces of Motoyui, paper cord for tying your hair but you can ask the people at the accommodation to assist you before passing through a checkpoint or in the area below the castle.

● Also bring a Chochin, paper lantern, candles, fire lighting tools and Kaichu Tsukeki, a parcel of strips of wood coated in in sulfur used as matches.

Even if you don't smoke tobacco you should carry these items with you. The Andon, fixed paper lamps, which light your hotel can go out easily and you may find yourself in a pinch. It's best to be prepared.

● A length of hemp rope. This extremely useful item can be used to wrap up your luggage and goods when you are staying at an inn.
● Inban, a copy of your house seal or name stamp. This is a wooden copy of your name stamp.

You would leave your house seal behind when setting out and use when writing letters back home. They can then compare the stamps to verify the letter's authenticity. This seal can also be used when exchanging money.

What You Should Bring on a Trip

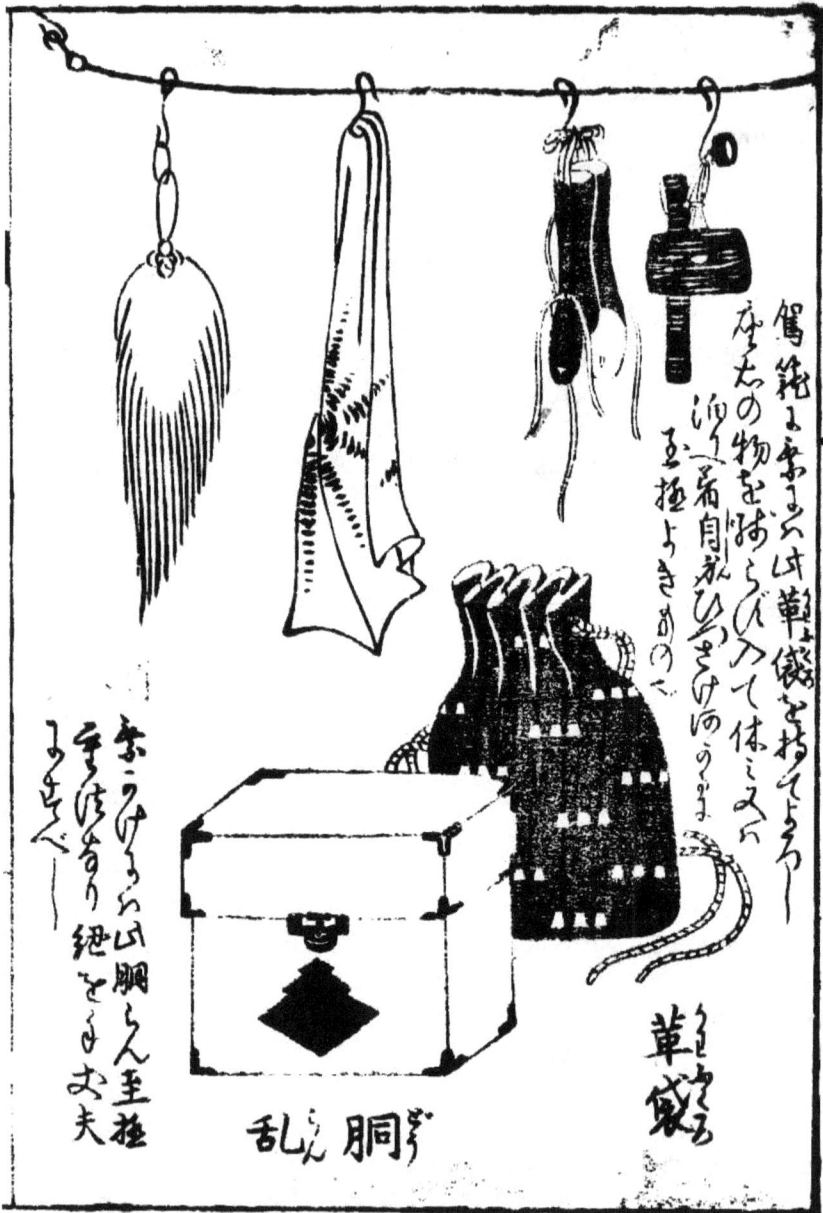

駕籠より外へは草鞋を持てよろしく
座右の物をはらくに入て休さ√に
沙〻帚月釵ひさきの沙のむ万
至極よきものに

まうけふうは胴らん至桓
手達らり紐をよ丈夫
まそぐ〳〵

乱しん 胴ぞう

草袋

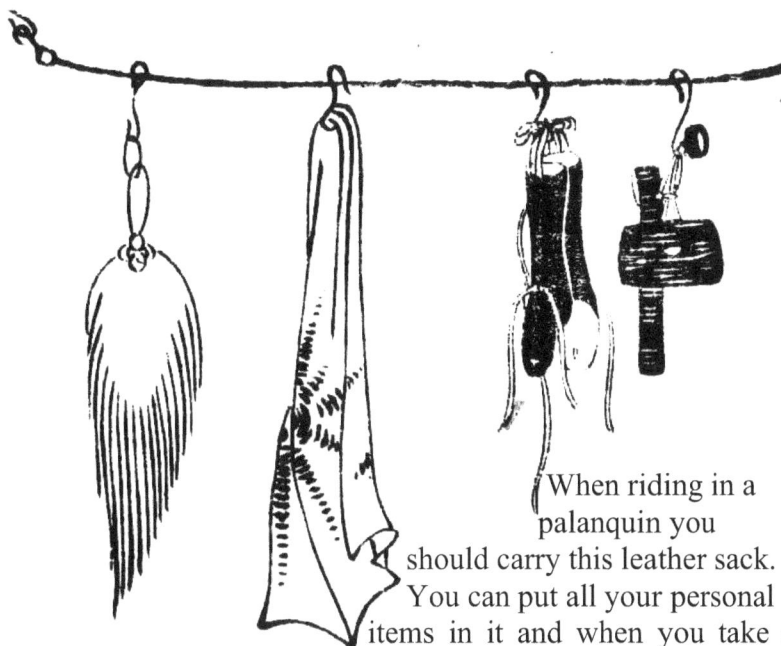

When riding in a palanquin you should carry this leather sack. You can put all your personal items in it and when you take a break or arrive at the inn you can carry all your things in this convenient sack.

Doran are useful way to carry things on a horse when you will also be riding. Doran "Waist Boxes for This and That" are a treasured item. If you wrap the lid in cord it is strong and easy to use.

If you carry a length of rope with a metal hook on the end, it will prove to be extremely useful.

How to keep a diary while on the road

While on the road if you happen up on a famous spot, some historic remains, a fine view or any other unusual sight, after asking about it be sure to write down that experience. Record the day and month, and write about what you saw as it occurs to you. If you happen to be inspired write a poem, Tanka short poem, Renka, poetic dialogue, or a Haiku be sure to write it down. Do not worry if you cannot finish it because the point of a diary is to write things as they occur.

In addition, if you are inspired to draw the mountains or rivers you see, simply record what you see. Later, after you return home you can make a final draft of the drawing. If you try to write perfect poems or draw perfect illustrations while on the road it will end up becoming troublesome to your journey. Frankly, you won't be able to do a good job. Keep this in mind.

Helpful Charts

Sunrise and sunset

○日の出入の事

正十節　卯ノ八分ニ出　酉ノ二分ニ入
正九節　卯ノ七分ニ出　酉ノ三分ニ入
二九節　卯ノ六分ニ出　酉ノ四分ニ入
二八節　卯ノ五分ニ出　酉ノ五分ニ入
三八節　卯ノ四分ニ出　酉ノ六分ニ入
三七節　卯ノ三分ニ出　酉ノ七分ニ入
四七節　卯ノ二分ニ出　酉ノ八分ニ入
四六節　卯ノ一時ニ出　酉ノ九分ニ入
五六節　卯ノ九分ニ出　戌ノ一時ニ入
五中　寅ノ九分ニ出　戌ノ二分ニ入
十中　卯ノ九分ニ出　酉ノ一分ニ入
十一節　辰ノ一時ニ出　酉ノ時ニ入
十一中　辰ノ一分ニ出　申ノ九分ニ入

Midday According to the Month

〇一年晝夜長短六ヲ割テノ大界

正月中　昼五十一コク半ヲ　夜四十九コク半ヲ
二月中　昼五十五コクヲ　夜四十四コク半ヲ
三月中　昼六十コクヲ　夜四十四コクヲ
四月中　昼六十四コク　夜三十六コク
五月中　昼六十五コク半ヲ　夜三十四コク半ヲ
六月中　昼六十四コク　夜三十六コク
七月中　昼六十コク　夜四十コク
八月中　昼五十五コク半ヲ　夜四十四コク半ヲ
九月中　昼五十コク半ヲ　夜四十九コク半ヲ
十月中　昼四十七コクヲ　夜五十二コクヲ
十一月中　昼四十五コク半ヲ　夜五十四コク半ヲ
十二月中　昼四十七コクヲ　夜五十二コク半ヲ

Cycles of the moon

月の出入の事

朔日・二日・三日・四日・五日・六日・七日・八日・九日・十日・十一日・十二日・十三日・十四日・十五日

Monthly Tide chart

〇潮の盈虚の事

138

How to Observe the Condition of the Sky
&
Old songs and sayings

- If rain starts to fall at around midnight, eight in the morning or around five in the evening it will likely rain for a long time. Further, if it begins to rain around ten in the morning or near six at night, then the weather will soon clear. Further, if it starts to rain around nine at night or at four in the morning from the direction the sun rises or around noon, then it will only be a sprinkle and soon stop. Further, if it starts to rain at about two in the afternoon or six in the evening as well as ten at night, then it will alternate in intensity before stopping after about half a day.

- When Kochi, the eastern spring, winds blow, rain is sure to fall. That being said, if an east wind blows during the rainy season or in the dog days of summer, that is a sign the rain falling will soon end.

  ○ If the east wind is gusting that is a sign the night will be clear.
  ○ If the wind is blowing from the northwest in spring or summer, it is a sign of rain.
  ○ If in autumn a west wind blows then rain will surely fall.
  ○ If a south wind blows in winter, then the ground will be covered in frost within three days.
  ○ A west wind or a northwest wind will bring clear skies. An eastern wind or a southern wind will bring rain.
  ○ If at sunset the sky is red or blue then the wind will rise. If at night the clouds are reddish then it will be clear. If the clouds are tumultuous then a strong wind will blow. If the clouds that appear before wind starts to blow don't have any trails extending out, then the rain will soon stop. If the clouds have become crimson and white then a great wind will blow.
  ○ Should the night become misty then strong wind will blow the following day.

○ If a shooting star streaks across to the east, then the wind will blow. If there is a halo around the moon at night and you can see stars in it, then rain will fall. If the lunar halo is doubled then a strong wind will blow. If you can see a bright light just as the moon sets, then rain will fall, however if the color is white then wind will blow. If you see a rainbow in the west in the morning then rain will fall within three days. If in the evening you see a rainbow in the eastern sky then the weather will turn fair. If bolts of lightning flash from all directions then expect a driving rain.

● If you want to know if rain is likely to fall check and see if the foundation stones your house rests on are damp.

   ○ If you see the mountains distinctly, then an east wind will blow. If the mountains are covered and can't be seen, then a north wind will blow.
   ○ Crows bathing in water is a sure sign that rain will fall.
   ○ If pigeons call out and their call is answered by other pigeons, then the weather will be clear. If there is no answering call, that is a sign of rain.
   ○ If the call of the Japanese black kite calls out in the morning, then rain will fall. If it calls in the evening it will be clear.
   ○ If the smoke from the cooking pot drifts idly downward then you should consider it likely rain will fall. If it rises straight up until it is out of sight, then it will be clear.

- You may be familiar with the terms Tenichi Taro, Hassen Taro, Doyo Saburo and Kanshiro.[27]

  There is a sixteen day period following Mizunotomi the intersection of Disposed Grass and Snake, the 30th day of the stems and branches cycle. The first day of this period is Tenichi Taro. If you take the 12 day period from Mizunoene, the intersection of Burden and Rat, until Mizunotoi, the intersection of Disposed Grass and Wild Boar and remove the day of the Ox, Dragon, Cow and Dog you end up with eight days. Those eight days are Hassen, Eight Specialized Days. The second day of Hasseen is Hassen Taro. The third day after Doyo, the hottest part of summer, is called Doyo Saburo. The fourth day after Kan, the coldest time of year, is called Kan Shiro. No matter which day these may fall on, if it starts to rain, the weather will turn bad.

- The climate and weather can change depending on the region you are in so it is tough to be specific. Generally speaking in the Kanto region if the wind blows from the west the weather will be clear. An east wind means rain will fall. In the western Kansai Region if a west wind blows then rain will fall. If the wind is out of the east then it will be clear. Therefore it depends on the region where you are. It is best to prepare yourself by asking locals.

---

[27] Tenichi Taro : The god of good fortune who descends to the northeast on the 46th day of the sexagenary cycle and completes a clockwise circuit. Traveling in the direction of Ten'ichijin is considered unlucky

Hassen Taro is on the 49th, 51st, 52nd, 54th, 56th, 57th, 58th or 60th day of the sexagenary cycle. Traveling on these days is inauspicious with a high probability of rain.

Doyo Saburo: The third day after the beginning of summer. If it is clear on this day it is a good time to plant crops. If rain should fall it is an unlucky day.

Kanshiro: Four days after the start of the cold season. An inauspicious day for wheat. If it is clear however, that year's crop will be bountiful.

百喜斎 ひからびし思ひは百舌の草ぐさのつつかけもの(突っ掛け)になるぞくやしき

I am drying up like the shrike hiding in the grass,
It's so disappointing knowing I'm destined to be impaled.
-Shrike by Hyakkisai Morikado
From *Myriad Birds: A Kyoka Poetry Competition*
Illustration by Kitagawa Utamaro 1790

鷹ならばうき名の外にぱつとたつ小鳥もをのがゑにしなる
べき

If I were a hawk I would soar above, with no thought of my
name and all the small birds would be my prey.

-*Hawk* by Akamatsu Kinkei
From *Myriad Birds: A Kyoka Poetry Competition*
Illustration by Kitagawa Utamaro 1790

Old Songs and Sayings

- If it is clear on Mt. Tsukuba or cloudy around Mt. Asama and a Mozu, or Japanese shrike, calls, you should set out on your journey even if it is raining.

- In May the wind blows from the west, in spring it blows from the south and in fall it blows from the north. You should consider wind blowing from the east to be a sign of rain.

- Spring brings north winds, winter brings south winds and the rest bring winds from the east, which are likely to bring dampness and rain.

- The kind of mist that rolls down the sides of mountains is called upward moving mist. Mist that seems to be climbing up from below is called Rain Will Fall Mist.

- I am particularly fond of those last two methods of predicting the weather. It is true that when the mist is rolling down, fine weather will follow and when the mist is rising, it will soon rain. I have personally checked this on a journey and found no error. These are easy to remember words. The first two old songs are based on the weather in the Kanto region.

No matter how close the Yahashi boat crossing may seem or how much in a rush you are, a Samurai should use the Seta Bridge.

This poem is referring to an area at the lowermost point of Lake Biwa, Japan's largest lake. There is one point towards the southernmost tip of the lake where you have the choice of traveling across by ship or taking a slightly longer walking route.

While faster, the boats can get caught in gusting winds blowing down of Mt. Hiei, which were strong enough to capsize the simple boats used for crossing. This poem cautions, *Though crossing by boat is faster, as a Samurai you should elect to travel the longer route for safety.* In this case, safety means being able to safely complete the mission assigned to you by your lord.

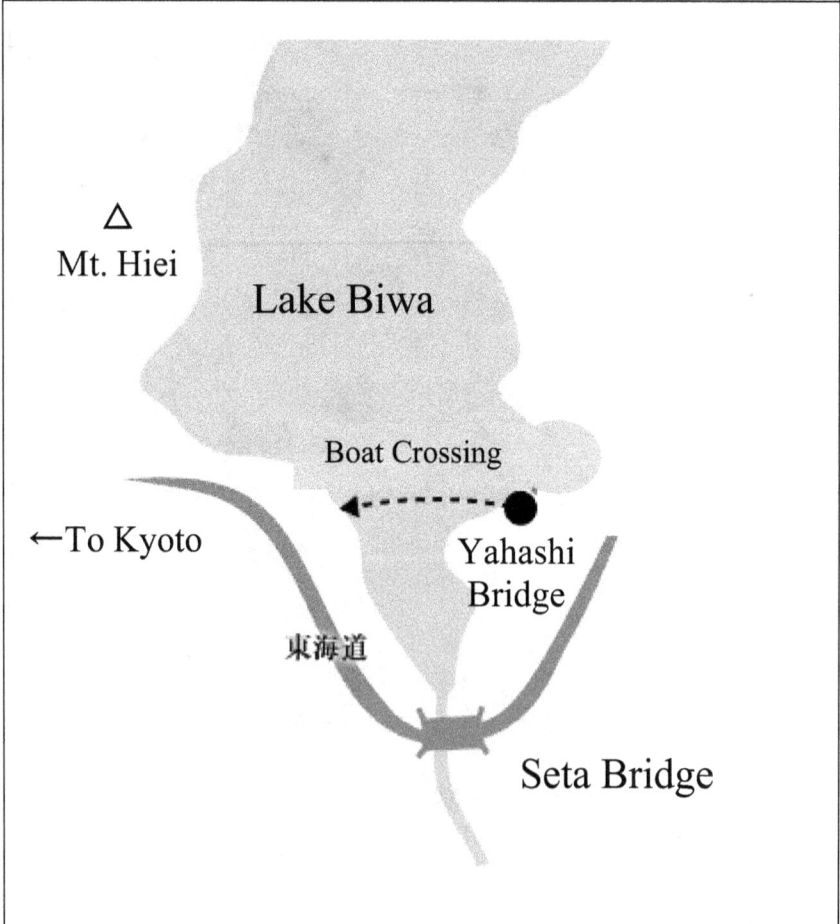

△
Mt. Hiei

Lake Biwa

Boat Crossing

←To Kyoto

Yahashi Bridge

東海道

Seta Bridge

Song of Things to Remember When Traveling

As soon as you arrive at your accommodation first orient yourself, second locate the bathroom, third lock the door and forth start a fire.

To travel with the attitude that you have complete freedom is an error. If you consider your time on the road as being full of restrictions you will end up enjoying yourself.

When embarking on a long trip you should commit yourself to brining the least amount of things as possible. Having a great deal of luggage is a recipe for disaster.

Some people embark on a trip thinking it will be all easy going. Know that when such people encounter a swollen river that has been rendered impassable, or other obstruction, it was preordained.

Those who depart early in the morning and check in to their accommodation early in the evening are far less likely to encounter trouble on their trip.

Avoid large meals while traveling. Instead take frequent rest breaks and eat several times a day.

People who arrive at their destination and then complain about the food likely have no understanding of the area, its people or customs.

Once you have experienced the land and customs in your destination, you will find even plain food is delicious.

Even if you are a Jogo, big drinker, when traveling avoid getting too deep in your cups. Its best to drink moderately and then Sake will act like a nice medicine.

When traveling, or at your destination, never take an unknown trail or cross an unknown river. This applies even if you are in a hurry.

If you are suddenly presented with the chance to take a ferry, consider carefully whether that will be faster or slower before deciding to board.

If it has been raining the whole day you have been traveling find accommodation as soon as the sky begins to lighten. If you wait until the sky is clear, all the good hotels will be taken.

Even if you are traveling with retainers and helpers, commit yourself to taking care of your own needs.

Remember that people who put on airs and act haughty while traveling will always encounter disaster.

If a fire breaks out near your accommodation, the first thing you should do is gather your things and get ready to leave. Next plan on carrying your luggage outside.

Watch your language when traveling and endeavor to keep your voice low. Boisterously stating your case for all to hear is something that should be avoided.

When on the road or at your destination you should never show off some skill you have. Though you may keep such talent hidden, you will eventually be recognized as being a person of skill.

Whether crossing a river or boarding or disembarking from a boat, keep firmly in mind that if you drop something it will be a disaster.

Never insult horse handlers, porters or palanquin bearers. No matter what work they do we are all humans in this world.

When traveling or at your destination even if you become angry, keep it in check. After some time has passed, quietly explain the situation.

If you are riding a horse that will also have your bags attached to it, be sure to check everything down to the smallest item. Before you mount the animal ensure your count is correct.

When setting off from your accommodation ensure you don't leave anything behind. Work together to check each other.

This *Song of Things to Remember When Traveling* is easy to remember so anyone can memorize it, so when you depart you will be prepared with valuable knowledge.

A Song for setting off on your journey

In your garden offer a branch of heather berries to the god Asuha, the god of travelers, to guard you until your return.
You cannot depend on fortune telling to determine a fortuitous day to depart. The best advice is to leave on a day you feel ready, and declare that your fortuitous day. Depart with that good feeling

Illustration of Hakutaku

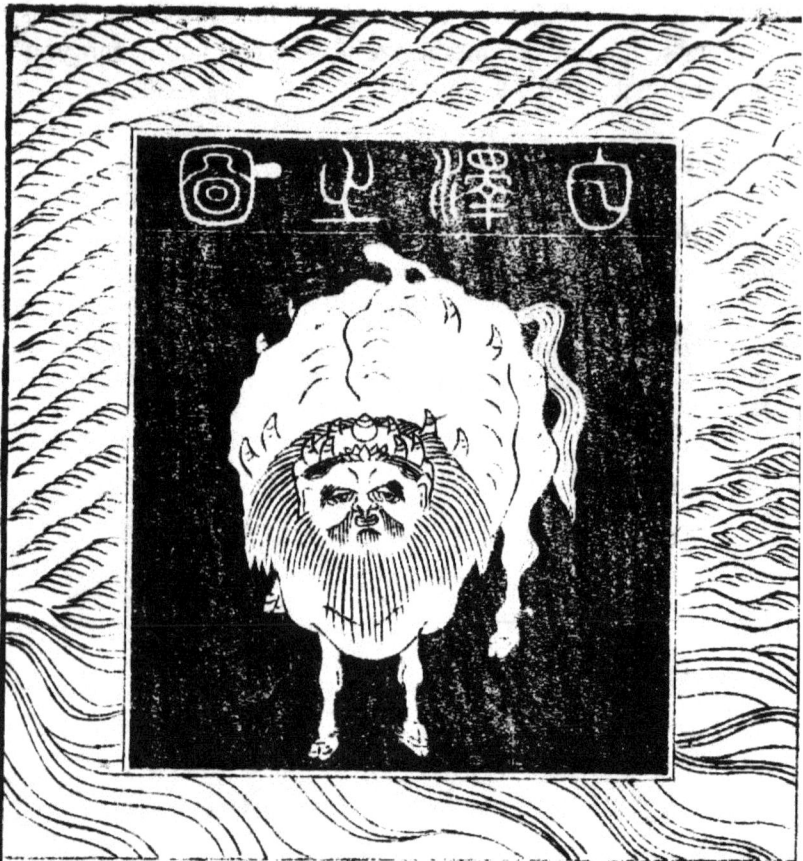

此白澤の圖成特
中もれが善事を
まるめそ惡事成
もれどを山海の
災雅病患をま
ぬの連開運昇
進の祥瑞ある
と古今云傳ふ
至て因而旅中や
最尊信あるぐ—

Illustration of Hakutaku

If you place this illustration of Hakutaku "White Marsh" inside your breast pocket, you will find yourself able to perform every action without trouble and you will not encounter any bad luck. You will be safe from disaster and illness both on the seas and in the mountains.

Your luck will open doors for you to succeed in life and it will be full of joyous profit. This has been told since days of old. So for the duration of your trip respect this image.[28]

---

[28] This mythical beast originated in China and made its way to Japan. Carrying its image was thought to act as a protective talisman since it knows the forms and habits of all supernatural creatures.

A 1785 illustration of Hakutaku 白沢避径図. It somewhat resembles a cow, but with multiple eyes and horns.

A True and Accurate Map of Japan Showing all the Domains As Well as the Southern Domains

A True and Accurate Map of Japan Showing all the Domains As Well as the Southern Domains

Map from the era of Emperor Yomei (540 ~ 587 AD,) the 31st Emperor of Japan, showing the Five Provinces and Seven Circuits. Under Emperor Monbu the 42nd Emperor (683 ~ 707 AD) the nation was divided into 66 countries.

A Guide to Japan's Onsen
292 Locations

Long ago in our country, before the advent of doctors or medicine, Onsen helped save people from illness or soothe their sorrow after losing a child. The gods Onamuchi no Mikoto along with Sukunai Hinano Mikoto traveled the whole country locating these hot springs, which people began to use as a way to heal illnesses. After that, people began using these baths as therapy no matter how high or low their status might be in society.

When I speak of Onsen, I am referring to the mysterious natural power they have to make the skin smooth, relax the joints, improve blood circulation and strengthen the operation of the organs. Thus, if you find an Onsen that works well on a particular illness, you can cure any illness without consulting a doctor and without taking any medicine. Therefore people that use hot springs therapy believe firmly in it and cherish this resource.

- The following list of Onsen in each domain of Japan is both for those seeking the revitalizing powers of the hot springs and, of course, for those seeking their therapeutic powers. You may end up partaking of the Onsen on the spur of the moment during the course of a pilgrimage or during a fun excursion. So, for easy reference, I have organized this list by each domain and included the nearby roads as well as the particular effects of each Onsen. I recommend you use this chapter as a reference as you follow the route, and check the book as you visit each site. If you happen to arrive in an area where you don't know the effect of the Onsen, be sure to question the locals carefully before you enter the therapeutic waters. The Onsen in a given area may or may not be effective in treating your illness or condition. It is important not to take this point lightly.
- Once you have arrived at an Onsen, you need to determine if it will treat your illness or condition effectively. After going into the Onsen once or twice, if you feel hungry and food tastes particularly delicious, you should consider that Onsen as having a good effect. On the other hand, if, after going into the Onsen once or twice, and your appetite doesn't

increase and your stomach feels full, then that Onsen probably does not suit your illness. Frankly, after you arrive at your destination, you need to find out all you can about the Onsen attached to your accommodation. Explain your medical needs carefully before entering the therapeutic waters. That being said, after going into the therapeutic waters two or three times you will probably naturally develop an idea of how they suit you.

- The way to use therapeutic waters is to use them 3 or 4 times a day for the first day or two. After that, if the Onsen suits you, try to enter the waters from 5 to 7 times a day. If you are elderly or have a general weakness of the body, then adjust the frequency accordingly. In addition, if you have a condition that has afflicted you for many years, you should understand that it won't be cured by one course of treatment at an Onsen. It will take several trips if not a period of one or two months of continuous use.

- Those using the hot springs, especially those using them for therapy, and even those who are healthy, should all be careful not to overeat, get extremely drunk, have sexual intercourse, or eat cold foods. When you get out of the heated water all your pores will be open and it is easy to get cold. So avoid exposing your body to the cold breezes in the mountains, chilling your feet in spring water or sleeping in a place with a strong breeze blowing across. Getting chilled after being in an Onsen is much more severe than getting chilled at any other time. You should exercise caution.

- The water in an Onsen should be hot and clear with the best ones having water clear enough to see the bottom. Onsen that are cloudy, lukewarm or have a strange color are not of high quality. That being said there are some Onsen that are cloudy and have unusual coloring but are not dangerous and, in fact, are quite pleasant to experience and treat illnesses effectively. So this rule isn't unconditional. In addition, understand that several Onsen hotels can use the hot waters welling up from one source. Since the therapeutic waters at each of these Onsen hotels can have different effects, you should carefully inquire at each hotel. No matter how famous an Onsen may be, it may or may not be appropriate to your condition or illness. I recommend you take care and make sure you get all the information you need.

- The following The Onsen of Japan section details 292 Onsen spread across 40 domains. There are of course a great many not listed here. However an exhaustive list would have been impossible. The reader should feel free to add any Onsen they visit to this book.

Onsen From all Domain
Within the Five Domains Adjacent to Kyoto

Yamato Domain
Musasi Onsen
Shio no Ha "Salty Leaf"

Settsu Domain
Arima Onsen
14 Ri from Kyoto
9 Ri from Osaka

Tada Onsen
About 1 Ri from Ikeda
Hitokura
In Hitokura Village

- The bathhouse at Arima no Yu, There is a Horse Onsen, is just one building. The "hot-water boat" or bathtub is about 114 cm deep 6.5 meters long and about 4 meters wide with a stone bottom. Bamboo tubes stick out from between the stones and hot water flows out of them. The water tastes very salty. The "hot-water boat" has a dividing wall of wooden planks in the center dividing it in two. The southern part is called Ichi no Yu, First Bath, and the Norther part is called Ni no Yu, Second Bath. There are twenty bath houses are referred to as the "20 Monks Chambers" and are divided into north and south. In addition, there are many other houses that rent rooms to travelers and are like small inns.

Arima Onsen with Mt. Narita in the background

In each of the hotels that make up the 20 Monks Chambers there are two women. The first is called the O-Yuna, Great Bath Attendant, but she unusually goes by the name Ka-ka, meaning "mama." The other is Ko-Yuna, Small Bath Attendant. She is usually a young lady. Each house uses the same nicknames generation after generation.

These two Yuna, Female Bath Attendants, inform the guests what order they will use the bath in. In addition, they also escort guests to and from the baths, so there is no need to worry about making a mistake.

This Onsen also uses Tome-yu, Onsen Stop, dividers. This is a curtain they pull across the Onsen so other guests cannot enter.

Ichi no Yu, First Bath

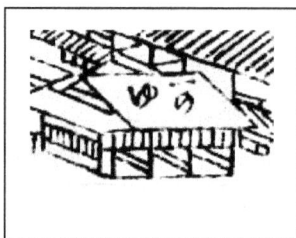

I have included the nickname for the Ko-Yuna, Small Bath Attendant. The O-Yuna, Big Bath Attendant, is always referred to as Ka-ka or "mama."

These are the names of the 20 Onsen hotels in this area along with the nickname for the Ko-Yuna, Small Bath Attendant.

Okunobo Inn - Summer Girl
Iseya Inn - Bamboo Girl
Goshonobo Inn - Evergreen Girl
Azakibo Inn - Drifting Girl
Shogiya Inn - Cedar Girl
Kakunobo Inn - Ivy Girl
Nikaibo Inn - Chestnut Girl
Daimon Inn - Dragon Girl
Wakasaya Inn - City Girl
Nakanobo Inn - Normal Girl

Ni no Yu, Second Bath

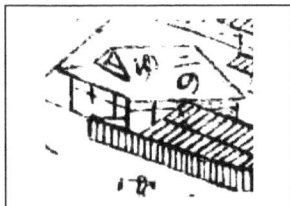

Ikenobo Inn - Pine Girl
Kawazakiya Inn - Grass Girl
Yasumitori Inn - Samurai Girl
Kawanoya Inn - Bright Girl
Hyoei Inn - Small Night Girl
Okuroya Inn - Fishing Rod Girl
Suisen Inn - Shortcut Girl
Getadaibo Inn - Iron Pot Girl
Somenya Inn - Wisteria Girl
Ginobo Inn - Early Times Girl

- There is a hot springs here known as the Jealous Onsen or Concubine Onsen in Yuhoncho Town. If a woman wearing make-up passes by this Onsen, the hot water begins to pour out in a furious torrent.
- Meimoku-yu, The Eye Onsen, is below Onsen Temple. It is effective for eye disease.
- Tada-yu, Many Fields Onsen, is also known as Wide Field Onsen. The bath is a square 15 meters on a side. In the center there is a divider separating the men's bath and the women's bath. The water for this Onsen is rather lukewarm when it arrives at the bath so they light a fire to heat it up.
- Hitokura-yu, One Storehouse Onsen, is in the middle of the mountains in Hitokura Village in the Tada region. This bath is heated with fire to make the therapeutic hot water.

Along the Tokaido Road

Ise
Komono Onsen

The water in this hot springs is only lukewarm since it is in the middle of the mountains and therefore mixed with water from the river that runs through the valley. It is heated with fire beforehand.

Tohto-umi
Mushiu Onsen
"Birthplace of Insects" Hot Spring

Kai
Kawaura Onsen
Shimobe Onsen
Narada Onsen
Enzan Onsen
Kurobera Onsen
Yumura Onsen

Izu Region
Atami Onsen

This Onsen is 7 Ri from Odawara. If you are traveling from Edo, a Tegata, travel permit is required at the Nebukawa checkpoint. There are many Onsen in Atamai.

Se-zaemon Onsen

If the flow of water is slow you can go beside it and if you call out in a whisper, the water flow will increase slightly. If you call out loudly, the water flow will bubble forth vigorously.

Nonaka-yu Onsen

This Onsen is beside Oyu Onsen in Uwamachi.

Hosai-yu Onsen

This Onsen is located in the north part of Shimomachi in Nonaka. If you shout, "Crazy monk Hosai, crazy monk Hosai!" it will make the waters bubble more vigorously. The volume of water will increase or decrease depending on how loudly or quietly you call out.

Kawara-yu Onsen
This is located to the south of Hosai-yu Onsen. Recently people seem to not use this hot springs.

Sui-yu Onsen
Located in the north of Honcho. This hot springs also seems to have been abandoned.

Furobo Onsen
This is beside Sui-yu.

Hashiri-yu Onsen
Also known as Dragon Onsen, this hot springs is about half a Ri from Atami. It is just south of the shrine to Gongen, a manifestation of a Buddha in the form of a Shinto Kami.
Kona Onsen
This Onsen is located 3 Ri down the Tokaido road from Mishima Postal Station near the Shimoda Kaido trail.

Shuzenji Temple Onsen
This lovely Onsen is located 5 Ri down the Tokaido road from Mishima Postal station.

Yoshina Onsen
Yoshina, which can be written either よし名 or 吉奈 is located 7.5 Ri from Mishima postal station.

About the Onsen in The Izu Region

- The water flowing into the Atami Onsen is extremely hot and it bubbles up and flows out six times a day. It is salty to the taste and beautifully clear. However, since the Onsen is near the shore and the air is full of cool salt spray the heat feels quite mild, and not at all intense.

  There are over a dozen hotels with Onsen in this area and for the most part they funnel the water from the source of the hot spring through wooden gutters.

  Also, Atami is famous for its spiritual power spots and scenic overlooks. In fact, there are too many to name here, however Higanezan, Golden Day Mountain is one of the finest in the land. To the southwest you can see Miho Matsubara, as well as Fuji River and to the north you can see Mt. Fuji, Mt. Ashitaka "Hawk's Foot Mountain," Mt. Futago "Twin Mountain," as well as the peaks of Mt. Amagi, Mt. Kanuki and the ridgeline of Ito. Additionally, on the sea you can make out the shapes of Hatsujima Island, Oshima Island and others. It almost seems as if you can see houses floating on the waves.

  Boats that are traveling from western regions to eastern regions have to pass across this area of ocean. In addition, travelers can find all manner of local specialties including the meat of wild beasts and fish, basically it is a shopper's paradise.

- The Onsen in Atami can treat palsy, convulsions, dizziness and lightheadedness, congestion in the chest, eye disease, headaches, backaches, bruises and beriberi (thiamine deficiency,) road rash, stumbling, bruises and sprains, bug bites, tapeworms, hemorrhoids, prolapsed anus, ulcers, skin conditions, wounds, gonorrhea, cuts, cramps and breathing difficulty. However, if you suffer from swelling you should not use these Onsen. If you have a toothache, the best treatment is to swirl the water around in your mouth several times.

- If you have any of the following diseases or conditions you should not go in the Onsen around Atami. If a person has swelling, intestinal swelling that makes the abdomen budge, leprosy, seizures, jaundice, people in a state of lethargy and other related illnesses then they should not use the Onsen.

- Shuzenji Temple Onsen has many different themed hot springs including Box Onsen, Stone Onsen, Stop Onsen, New Onsen and Vajra Onsen. They vary in temperature and treat different sorts of ailments and injuries so the user can decide which one suits them best.
- Yoshina Onsen have very mild waters and are therefore easy to use. Your entire body will relax as your spirit is soothed. Even if you sink in up to your shoulders you soon lose track of time and never really feel hot. Elderly people, housewives, those with stiff backs, hemorrhagic lesions, lower abdominal pain, palsy or those suffering from a general weakness of the body and others will benefit from the hot springs in this area which gradually heat the body.

Shuzenji Temple on Mt. Shoro in the Kamo Area of Izu domain is notable since the mountain view recalls Mt. Ro in China. The Chinese Zen priest Rankei Doryu (1213-1278) who traveled to Japan in 1246, named Mt. Shoro. The temple contains a portrait of the Song dynasty emperor Riso, among other rare and wonderful items. It is an extremely lovely view and I recommend you visit it.

Sagami Region

Hakone Yumoto "Source of the Hot Springs"
1.5 Ri[29] from Odawara. There are 9 resorts.
Tonosawa Onsen – 12 Cho[30] from Yumoto, 12 resorts.
Miyanoshita Onsen – 1.5 Ri from Tonosawa, 8 resorts.
Dogashima Onsen – about 10 Cho towards the valley, 6 resorts.
Sokokura Onsen – down the road from Dogashima, 4 resorts
Kiga Onsen – a short trip from Sokokura, 3 resorts
Serinoyu Onsen – 1 Ri 16 Cho from Sokokura, 5 resorts
Zenjo Onsen, also known as Ubako Onsen – 5 Ri from Odawara, no actual resort establishments.
Kogome Onsen, also known as Childbirth Onsen or Inner River Onsen.

---

[29] One Ri 里 is 3.927 kilometers or 2.44 miles.
[30] One Cho 町 is 109 meters or 357.6 feet.

About the Onsen in The Sagami Region

- There are many kinds of Onsen and they can treat sexually transmitted diseases, discomfort related to hemorrhoids, back pain, spasms and also the waters are effective on cuts.
- The waters of Tonosawa Onsen are particularly effective on headaches, dizziness, chills in the lower body, bruises, sprains, mouth and tongue pain, boils, asthma and bloody saliva.
- The waters of Miyanoshita Onsen are effectively treat discomfort related to hemorrhoids, gonorrhea, skin disorders and tapeworms.
- The recuperative and healing effects of the waters at Dogashima Onsen are the same as those of Miyanoshita Onsen.
- Sokokura Onsen waters treat discomfort related to hemorrhoids as well as prolapsed colon and all pain and conditions related to the anus. That is why male prostitutes frequent these hot springs for treatment.
- Kiga Onsen treats numbness in the hands and feet, muscle and bone seizures, headaches, chest congestion, bruises, pulled muscles, sprains, gout and so on.
- Serinoyu Onsen treats beriberi, muscle spasms, tuberculosis, body odor, bed-wetting, gonorrhea women's gonorrhea and cuts.
- The effects of the rest of the Onsen are unknown.

The above Onsen in the Hakone area of Sagami Domain are about 20 Ri from Edo. The roads along the way are not dangerous and your destination is just before the checkpoint station. Therefore, men and women, young and old currently living in the capital can all make the journey for treatment at these Onsen. In particular the scenery around Enoshima Island, Kamakura City and Kanazawa City is particularly striking and refreshes the body and spirit. Overall this area is a fantastic health spa retreat.

It is interesting to note that the Seven Hot Springs of Hakone are all of top quality, and it is as if those areas are in competition with each other. Since Atami is only separated from Hakone by 7 or 8 Ri, the question of which is the more famous comes down to the effectiveness of the Onsen in each area. Due to its proximity to Edo this area is the most active area for hot springs resorts.

Urami Waterfall in Mt. Nikko
"There are many monkeys here."

Also in this area:

Muasahi
Ogawauchi Onsen – On the border of Kai Domain. Effective for cuts.

Awa
Umasugi Onsen
Joriku
Fukuroda Onsen – At the base of Moonbreak Mountain. The water is heated by fire before being pumped into the Onsen.

Along the Tosando Trail "Eastern Mountain Circuit"

Hida Region
Shinno Region
Translator's Note: The list of Onsen has been abbreviated since it contains no details.

Ueno Region
Ikoho Onsen
The waters at this Onsen treat sexually transmitted diseases, tuberculosis, any kind of cut as well as irritation. The Ikoho Onsen along with the neighboring Kusatsu Onsen are both excellent and it is hard to determine which is better. Some afflictions are better treated at Ikoho while other afflictions are better treated at Kusatsu. It depends on your condition. Thus, even though both are in the same region they both remain busy with guests. This is very similar to how Hakone and Atami compare with each other.

Shimoya Region

Nikko Sanchuzenji Temple Onsen
There are 3 Onsen here and it is located 3 Ri from Nikko Hatsuishi Town. All the Onsen here are excellent. Since it is a cold region you can travel there from around mid-March until the end of September. Those taking Onsen therapy in the summer should be sure to bring proper clothing as it is cold in the morning and evening.

Tenneiji Temple Onsen

*There are approximately 20 resorts in this area and each resort
has about two baths.*

Nasu Onsen

The Onsen in Nasu can treat a great many illnesses, however for those that have been bitten by the Mamushi pit viper will find the hot springs therapy will immediately relieve the pain of such bites. The scar will heal and you will suffer no lingering aftereffects.

Rikuoku & Aizu Region

There are many Onsen in this area which is about 65 Ri from Edo. They are mainly west of White River.

Tenneiji Temple Onsen

Tenneiji Temple Onsen is about 1 Ri east of the town at the base of Aizu Wakamatsu Castle. It is located in Tennei village in the mountains. There are about a dozen Onsen in this area which is near the source of the hot springs. All of them are large scale Onsen.

The water all comes from one source and is diverted to over a dozen resorts. However, each hot springs in these resorts has its own characteristics and the heat of the water can vary. As I mentioned before, find the Onsen that suits your illness and take hot springs treatment there.

The water in the Onsen in this area is extremely clear and pure. It is like a beautiful mirror and the Onsen in this area are all of such excellent quality they can be said to be the best in Japan.

In addition, in the middle of the town there is a Soyu, Open Onsen. It is used by travelers as well as landscapers and woodcutters. The water in this area isn't particularly hot when compared to other areas however, it makes your skin soft and treats a variety of illnesses.

The river below the resort area is called Yukawa, Hot Springs River. Here and there you can find hot water bubbling up in the middle of the river, creating Onsen. One of those is called Mesenjo, Eye Cleaning Onsen. You can find it by looking for the round, slightly indented rock in the middle of the river. It is said the water bubbling from that spot will cure eye diseases.

In addition, there is an Onsen at the bottom of the waterfall at the base of the mountain. It is called Saruyu, Monkey Onsen. The waterfall is called Monkey Onsen Waterfall.

The roads around this area are steep mountain roads. As Onsen River flows down the mountain, many waterfalls are formed. Of note is the Fushimi Waterfall. It falls in two powerful streams known as Male and Female.

About half-way up the mountain above this waterfall there are two or three Onsen resorts. These resorts are known as Waterfall Onsen. The water in these resorts is spectacularly clear and can treat a variety of diseases. Further, the views of nature from these spots are incomparable and no artist's rendering could do them justice.

About 7 Ri northwest of Aizu Wakamatsu there is the village of Atsushio, or "Hot Salt," that has many Onsen.

Regarding the Sekisho, Checkpoints, Around the Country[31]

Be sure to take care of your Dochu Tegata, or Travel Permit. Before going to the Sekisho, or Checkpoint, be sure to stop at one of the tea houses nearby to ready your documents. Then proceed to the Checkpoint to present your document to the official.

If you just walk right up to the checkpoint you will have to search about in your pockets, no doubt pulling out packs of tissue paper and so on. Clearly you will not be prepared.

You should also prepare Women's Travel Permits the same way. If you are unsure of what to do ask an official at the Checkpoint.[32]

---

[31] The list of 53 checkpoints has been abbreviated since there was no information.

[32] A Sekisho, or checkpoint, was a facility posted at important sites along main roads to collect fees and perform inspections. While they were common in Japan from the 12th through the late 16th centuries, Oda Nobunaga ended the practice in the 1570s. The checkpoints were re-instated by the Tokugawa Shogun in the early 1600s, for general security as well as to guard against the military ambitions of the various Daimyo.

The two main purposes of the checkpoints were to restrict the transport of matchlock rifles and control the movement of women. Specifically, the Bakufu government wanted to prevent insurrection by controlling the flow of weapons and to watch the movement of the wives and children of Daimyo, since they were required to live with the Daimyo in Edo one year out of every three.

A Daimyo sending his wife back to his domain may signal the beginning of an insurrection, though it could also be a kidnapping. While all travelers had to have a travel permit, the ones for women were more detailed and the inspections were stricter. For example, they had to define the "type of woman." The documentation was called an Onna Tegata 女手形, woman's travel permit. These would list a female traveler as: Zen nun, nun, young girl under 15, crazy woman, woman with her hair cut short or the corpse of a woman. In order to bring a Teppo, or matchlock, into Edo you had to have a 鉄砲手形 Teppo Tegata, or official permit.

Sekisho were abolished in the second year of Meiji 1869.

Top: Travel Permit for 5 men from 1851
Bottom: Transcription into standard Kanji

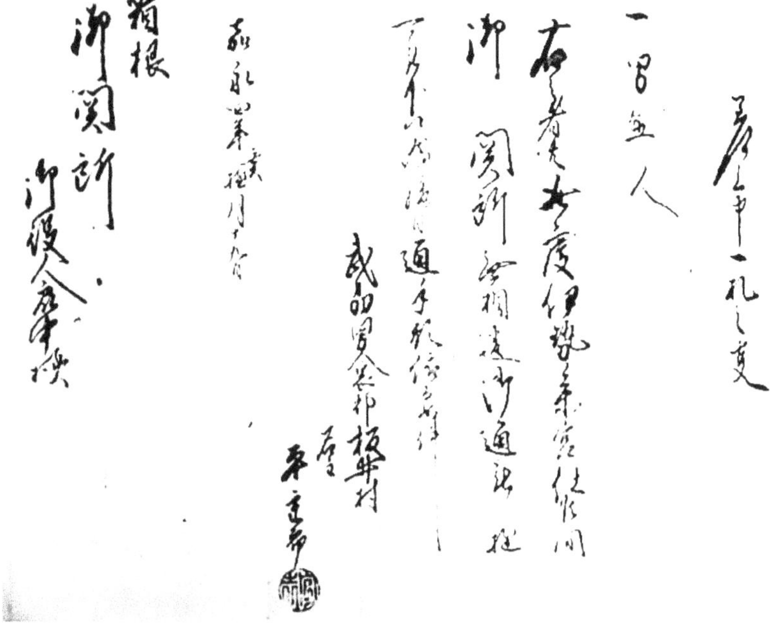

差上申一札之事

一　男五人

右之者共、此度伊勢参宮仕候間、
御　関所無相違御通被　遊可被下
候、為後日通手形依而如件

武州男衾郡板井村

名主

平重郎㊞

嘉永四年亥極月十九日

箱根
御関所
御役人衆中様

171

Top: Travel Permit for 5 men from 1851
Bottom: Transcription into standard Kanji

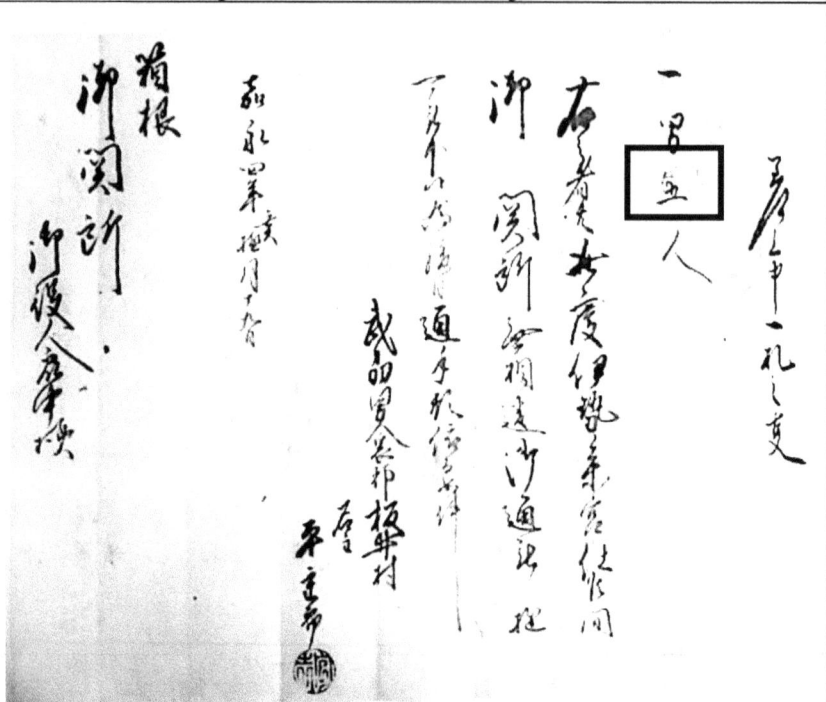

To Whom It May Concern at Hakone Sekisho

This letter is submitted for your approval.

The five men before you are on a pilgrimage to Ise Shrine. Please allow them to pass safely through the Sekisho, further allow them to pass through again on their return. This is the purpose of this Tsuko Tegata.

Head of Obusumagun Region Itai Village
Hirashige Roh December 19th Kanei 4 (1851)

There is a Hanko, or seal, directly on the number "five" 五 to prevent the number from being changed.

Top: Woman's Travel Permit from 1829
Bottom: Transcription into standard Kanji

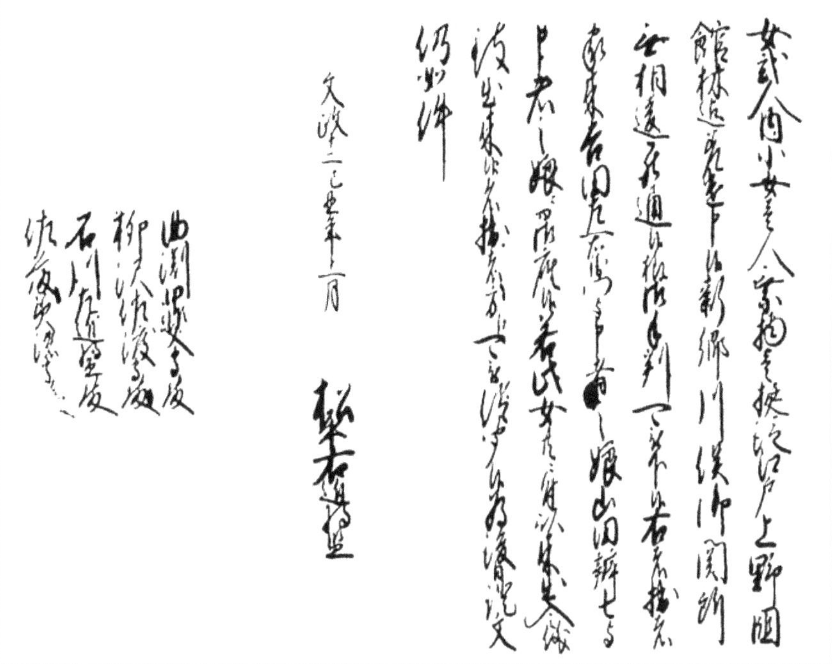

女弐人、内小女壱人、乗物壱挺、従江
戸上野国館林迄差遣申候、新郷川俣御
関所無相違罷通候様、御手判可被下
候、右者拙者家来・吉田左一右衛門与
申者之娘、山田弁七与申者之娘二而御
座候、若此女共二付、以来出入之儀、
致出来候者、拙者方江可被仰聞候、為
後日証文仍如件

文政十二己丑年十一月　松平右近将監

曲淵甲斐守殿
柳沢佐渡守殿
石川左近将監殿
佐藤美濃守殿

Top: Woman's Travel Permit from 1829
Bottom: English translation

There are two women, one of which is young. They are taking a boat from Edo up to Tatebayashi in Ueno Domain. Please allow them permission to pass safely through the checkpoint at Shingo Kawamata.

The two women are the daughter of my retainer Yoshida Saichi Uemon and the daughter of my retainer Yamada Benshichi. If there are any issues regarding these two passing through the checkpoint feel free to ask me.

This document also serves as their return pass.

Matsudaira Ukon 3rd head of Ueno Tatebayashi
November of Bunsei 12 (1829)

Top: Gun Transport Permit from 1721
Bottom: Transcription into standard Kanji

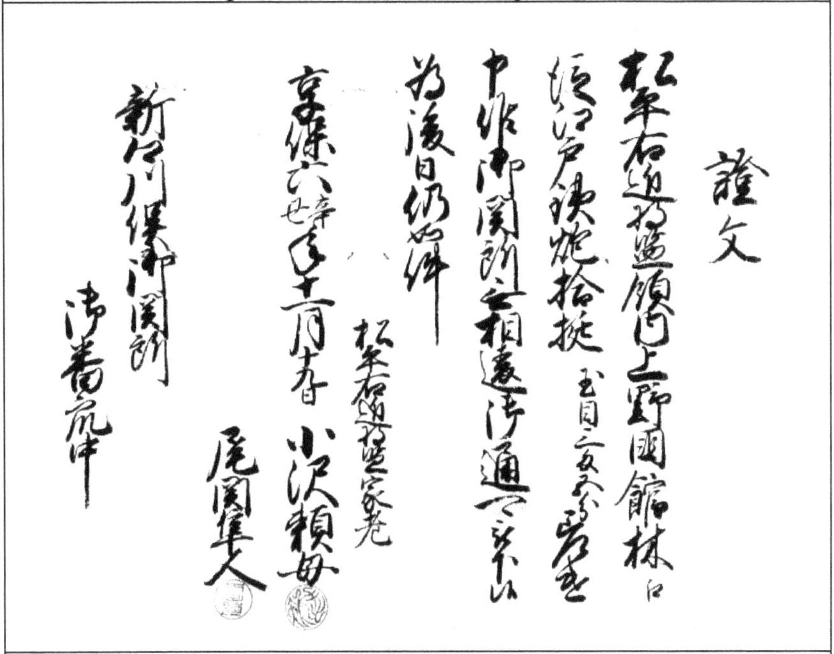

証文

松平右近将監領内上野国館林江、従三江戸二鉄炮拾挺、玉目三匁
五分差遣申候、御関所無三相違二御通可被下候、為三後日二、
仍如件

享保六辛丑年十一月十九日

新郷川俣御関所
御番衆中

松平右近将監家老
小沢頼母印

尾関隼人印

Top: Gun Transport Permit from 1721
Bottom: Transcription into standard Kanji

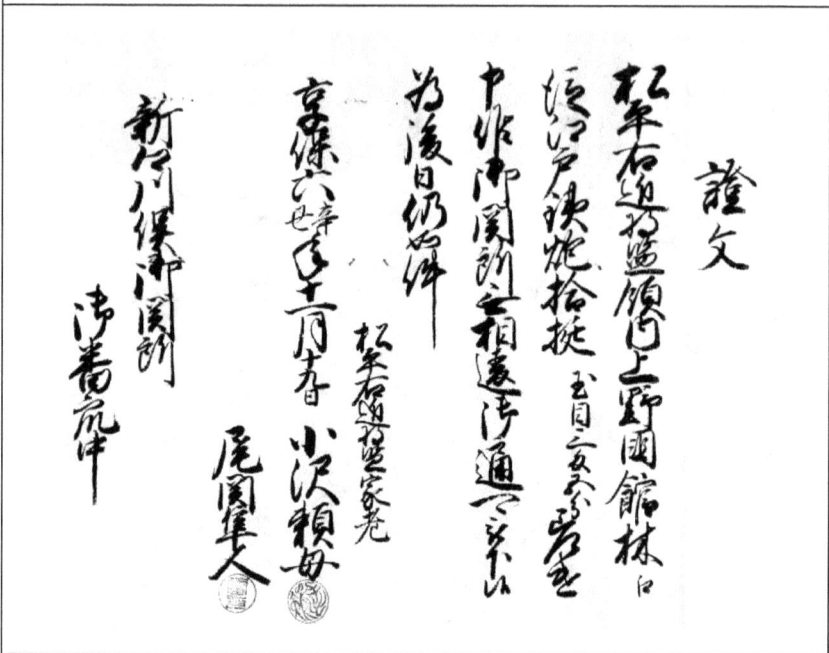

To Whom It May Concern at Shingokawamata Sekisho Checkpoint

This is a letter of transport for 10 Teppo, or Matchlock Rifles, with 3 Monme 5 Bun, 13 gram, ammunition. They will be transported from Edo to the lands under control of Matsudiara Ukon in Tatebayashi, Ueno Domain.
Please allow them to pass without delay through your Sekisho Checkpoint and return through at a later date.

Elder Advisor Matsudaira Ukon
November of Kyoho 6 (1721)

Additional Costs Along the Tokaido, Nakasendo, Nikko Dochu, Koshu Dochu and Oshu Dochu[33]

Additional costs for the following at each station:
For hiring a Honma, luggage horse
For hiring a Kara-shiri, horse for riding and luggage
For hiring Ninsoku, a porter

---

[33] The remainder of this book consists of lists of various sorts. Since they are lists of numbers I will just introduce the sections.

The Proper Trail to Take from Nihonbashi in Edo to all Areas
Distance and Prices for Porters for:
53 Stations on the Tokaido
Saya Mawari
69 Stations of the Kisoji Trail
Distances to various places

For hiring a Honma, luggage horse
For hiring a Kara-shiri, horse for riding and luggage
For hiring Ninsoku, a porter

33 Famous Spiritual Images of the Kannon in Western Japan

西國三十三所

観音霊場地名

一番　紀伊国　那智山
二番　同　紀三井寺
三番　同　粉河寺
四番　和泉国　槇尾寺
五番　河内国　葛井寺
六番　大和国　壺坂寺
七番　同　同寺
八番　同　長谷寺

34 Famous Spiritual Images of the Kannon in Chichibu

秩父三十四所

観音霊場地名

一番　四万部　妙音寺
二番　大棚　真福寺
三番　岩木　常泉寺
四番　荒木　金昌寺
五番　　　語歌寺
六番　萩　卜雲寺
七番　牛伏　法長寺
八番　青苔山　西善寺

33 Famous Spiritual Images of the Kannon in Bando

坂東三十三所

観音霊場地名

一番　相州　鎌倉　杉本寺
二番　同　鎌倉　岩殿寺
三番　同　三浦　田代堂
四番　同　長谷寺
五番　同　足柄郡　飯泉
六番　同　飯山　長谷寺
七番　同　金目　光明寺
八番　同　星谷　星谷寺

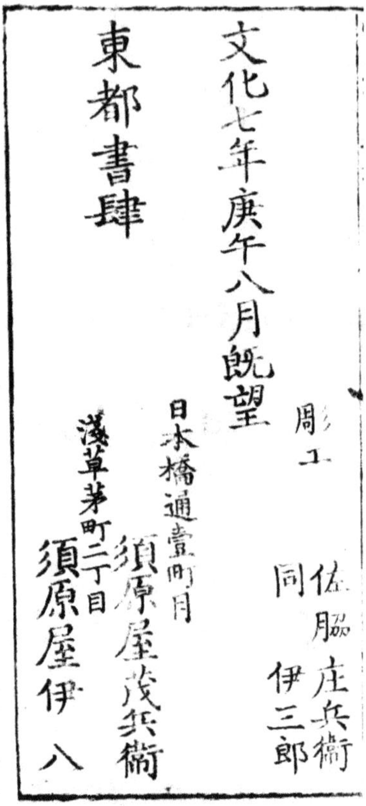

文化七年庚午八月既望

東都書肆

彫工

日本橋通壹町目
須原屋茂兵衛

淺草茅町二丁目
須原屋伊八

佐脇庄兵衛
同
伊三郎

How to Travel Safely in Japan
End

Published in August of Bunka 7 (1810)
Illustrated by Sawaki Shobe & Sawaki Isaburo

Excerpt from:
A Rough Outline of How to Raise Healthy Children

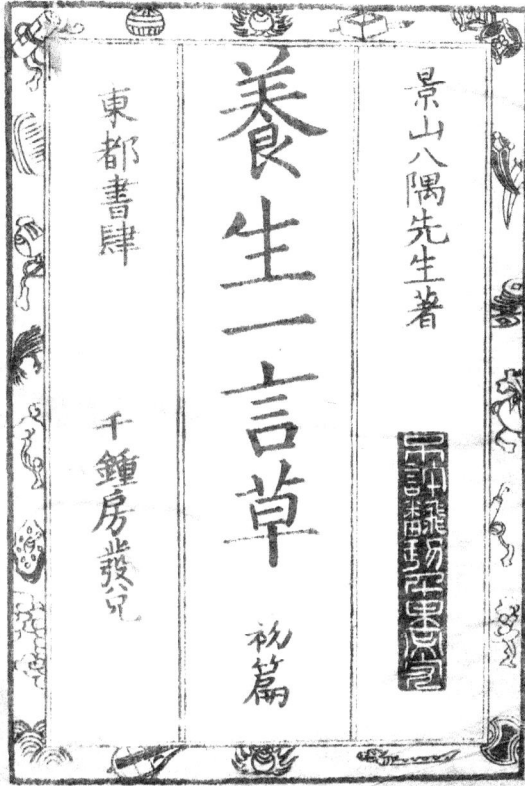

景山八隅先生著

東都書肆

千鍾房發兌

養生二言草

初篇

By Kageyama Yasumi Sensei (Yasumi Roan)
Published 1830

Translator's Introduction

In the 2nd Year of Tenpo (1830) Yasumi Roan published an illustrated book titled *A Rough Outline of How to Raise Healthy Children.* This is a translation of one of the chapters titled *Children's Toys* that outlines the education curriculum for children growing up. It is interesting for many reasons but I enjoyed the early definitions of martial arts and decided to include it.

Kites

Children's Toys

The games played by children follow a natural progression. A boy or girl is born, and eventually they learn how to sit up. They learn how to crawl, they start teething, start walking and begin to say the names of things. At some point your child will stop breast feeding and begin to chew food on their own.

Your child will go from 3 years old to 4, 5, 6 and 7 years old. Girls and boys will each begin to play their own sorts of games because they have developed qualities given to them by the heavens. While initially babies can only squeeze their hand into fists and make small sounds, eventually they become able to clap their hands, play steal-the-child or play blindfold the demon.

Girls will make and play with silk Temari balls or play Hago (Japanese badminton.) Boys play with Hamayumi (small bow and arrow) and different kinds of kites. These types of play are all done at different times during your child's development. If children do not learn how to play games they will not digest food well and their blood circulation will be poor. Thus if you wish to raise healthy young children their main activity should be playing games.

Thus, you will find children that play a lot of games digest their food well, urinate and defecate without trouble, have good blood circulation, have vitality, and overall do not suffer from illness. Therefore children playing a lot of games when young directly correlates to those same children becoming strong youth. This applies no matter what their social status Shi-No-Ko-Sho 士農工商, Samurai, farmer, craftsman or merchant and no matter what art they pursue. [34]

---

[34]**Shi**– Samurai (around 10% of the population) were the rulers, superior in both their status and the example they set.

No – Farmers (around 80% of the population) were second because they produced the food necessary for society.

Ko – Craftsmen and artisans (around 5%) were placed next since they made things for people to use.

Sho – Merchants (around 5%) were ranked the lowest since they sold things made by others.

In addition about 1% of the population was in the priesthood and another 1% were considered outcasts.

子とろとろ
Steal the Child

羽子
Hago or Yarihago (Japanese badminton.)

子とろとろ
Steal the Child

To play steal the child, one person stands on the left and is the "devil." The first person on the right is the "parent" who stands with arms outstretched, blocking the devil. All the other players line up behind the parent and hold onto waists or shoulders. The goal of the devil is to catch the child at the end of the chain. The parent moves to stay in front of the devil and protect the children.

羽子
Hago or Yarihago (Japanese badminton.)

Hago is played with wooden boards shaped like a fan and a shuttlecock made of the nut of a washnut tree with feathers attached. The boards are often painted colorfully and displayed in the house. The image above is an Edo Era Hagoita, Hago racket.

Calligraphy

Tenarai
Writing Lessons

Your child should begin taking lessons in writing around the age of 6 or 7. This is generally the recommendation most parents follow.

Lessons should involve facing the teacher's writing table, grinding the ink stone until writing ink is made, watching the teacher demonstrate and then move their own brush as their teacher did. During these lessons they learn how to draw up and focus their mental energy. It is their first experience in the teacher student relationship. They learn how to show proper respect to their mother and father.

Children should first learn to write all 48 letters of the Hiragana alphabet that they learned from the Iroha, Japanese Alphabet Song. Next they should learn the numbers from 1 ~ 10 as well as north, south, east, west and all the directions in between. This will lay a foundation for memorizing information.

Reading and Lectures

Reading and Lectures

When your child turns 7 or 8 they should begin with a study of the rich and the poor, meaning the study of the class system. You should begin by finding a teacher for your child. Reading lessons include instruction in manners and posture beyond those that are taught during writing practice. They will also learn how to enter a room and greet people as well as the proper way to offer farewells when departing. Children will learn about how to speak to people who rank above and below them in status. They will gradually develop an understanding of filial piety. Once they are conscious of the necessity for loyalty, they will have achieved the first step in their lessons on behavior and etiquette.

At this stage your children will be rising early every day, going before their teacher and reciting lines. As they expel their voices their chests will expand with confidence. Their blood will circulate with vitality and they will eat well, thus forming a moral foundation that will last all their lives. This is the first step.

Manners

Manners and Discipline

So then as was mentioned before, your children have begun studying writing and readings in earnest and proper greetings and farewells can be performed without hesitation. The next step is to study the six arts, rites, music, archery, chariotry, calligraphy and mathematics as well as Chinese poetry, classical Japanese poetry, poetic dialogue, and Haiku.[35] There are others as well.

However, in order to successfully learn the above arts it is necessary to first study the proper etiquette used in each of them. In other words your children must begin to study the Ogasawara School of manners and etiquette. If your children study this school they will of course learn how talk and interact with people while sitting and standing but will also help them develop their own understanding of the differences between the classes.

A thorough understanding of the Ogaswara School material will mean their attitude will be correct and they will have a resolute spirit.[36] Their appearance will become more beautiful day by day. This is one of the most important lessons for the development of your children and should not be ignored.

---

[35] These are the "six arts" first introduced in the Zhou Era in China (1122–256 BC),
1. Rites 禮
2. Music 樂
3. Archery 射
4. Chariotry 御
5. Calligraphy 書
6. Mathematics 數

[36] The Ogasawara School was founded in the Kamakura Era (1185 ~ 1333.) The school's martial arts focused on archery and horsemanship, however they had many ceremonial rituals for every aspect of life. The teachings of Ogasawara school eventually became the standard to teach manners and discipline.

The Bow

Kyujutsu
Archery

Having studied writing, reading, etiquette and so on, the next topic is one that Samurai quite enjoy, archery and equestrian arts. In particular Yumi, the bow, is the first weapon to be studied. Initally, children learn how to draw the bow, then they learn how to shoot into a Makiwara, or straw bale. After children have trained extensively on Makiwara and developed some skill they move onto Mato, targets. Eventually they are able to shoot from horseback and reliably hit birds and beasts and so on. As their strength and skill increases, they become proficient in all areas of archery.

When doing archery you should calm your spirit, allow your chest and abdomen to expand and you must place power in the spot below your navel. Since controlling breathing is essential to archery, by becoming adept at it some people say, "Archery will help you to learn other martial arts." This is incorrect, as *the way of the bow* is the fundamental art of the Samurai upon which all others are built.

Horseback Archery

Horse

Joba
Equestrian Arts

Joba, the equestrian arts, feature predominantly in Samurai households and many hours are devoted to training it. Children growing up in such a household should do nothing other than train in this art. Riding through the mountains and crossing rivers requires a certain amount of spirit. Above all else, your spirit and your hips are the fundamental elements of horseback riding. Thus, famous riders are able to break even the wildest of horses and ride them in any conditions wherever they please. Moreover, they can ride distances of twenty or even thirty Ri in a single day. Despite this they remain alert and their horse does not suffer from exhaustion. This is due to the power of the rider's spirit and hips.

Initially, children should practice on a wooden horse and focus on how to handle the bridle. Learning 100 techniques on a wooden practice horse will allow you to reap great rewards. Since the equestrian arts encourage the circulation of your blood and vitality, it will enable you to live a long life free of disease.

Water Training

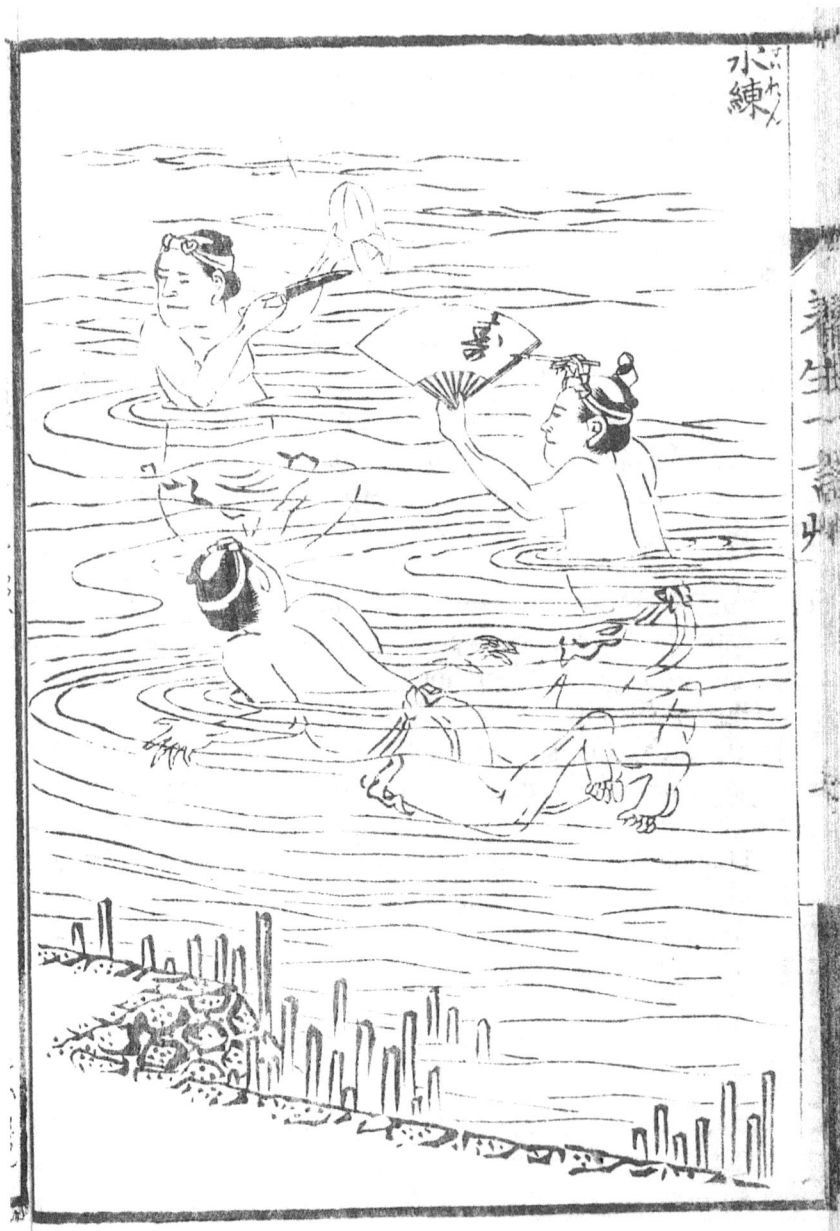

Suiren
Water Training

Training in water is enjoyed by Samurai in every domain in Japan. Depending on the area some swim in clear water while some swim in cloudy water or in ocean water by the sea. However, Samurai that train swimming in the ocean sink in river water and those that train in river water find they can't swim in the ocean. It is the basic principle.

By training in swimming, Samurai learn to write calligraphy on a folding fan, peel a melon, or eat a tray of food. There are many other techniques as well. Since these skills can't be learned on land, those that seek to be Samurai must all, without exception, experience this training.

There are many different schools that teach Suiren, Water Training. Each of them is slightly different and they use names like, Consecutive Swim, Floating Swim, Distance Swim, Resting Swim, Shoals Swim or Standing Swim, all of which are effective methods.

You may end up using these skills while on a trip as you may have to cross rivers on foot, cross by boat or temporary bridge. You may encounter a narrow bridge consisting of a bamboo pole for your feet and only the ropes on either side for balance. Also, it is possible you may inadvertently fall into the water when traveling by the beach, or the side of a lake or pond.

In addition, if you are out hunting with your hawk and a great rainstorm darkens the sky, even an experienced hunter can slip and fall into a body of water. A person not familiar with swimming would be in danger.

Riding Horses in Water

Suiba
Riding Horses in Water

Suiba is the art of crossing a body of water with a horse. You should allow spring water to cover a wide area of your garden and practice there. Riding horses in water is quite different from riding horses on land and presents many challenges, however those seeking to be Samurai should focus on steadily developing their skill.

Keep in mind the image of the great historical figures like the 12th century Samurai Sasaki Takatsuna and Kajiwara Kagesue who raced each other across the Uji River with their horses, each striving to be the first to engage the enemy in the 1184 battle of Uji. There are countless other warriors from both Japan and China renowned for their ability to ride horses through water.

Sword Drawing

Iai
Sword Drawing

Iai is when you and your opponent draw close to each other, then, in a flash, draw swords and cut in the blink of an eye. It is said an adept practitioner can wait until they are 1 or 2 Sun, 3 ~ 6 centimeters, from their target. They can draw an O-Dachi, the largest of swords. In a room only four tatami mats in size they can draw a 5 Shaku, 180 cm, sword without touching the surrounding walls.

The deftness with which they apply power when drawing and sheathing is spectacular to behold and their movement is so fast it doesn't register on the eye of the viewer. Iai is the art of drawing either of your two swords whether you are walking, standing, sitting or lying down. There are many different schools of sword drawing.

Sword Fighting

Kenjutsu
Swordsmanship

Kenjutsu, or swordsmanship, is the primary martial art practiced by Samurai families. Developing skill in this art should be the main focus of everyone as a matter of course. There are many different schools of this art and numerous branches within each school however, despite the many different styles, the underlying teaching is the same.

If it is a day you will be training swordsmanship, approach it by being sure to eat a proper amount, relax and focus your energy. You should be aware that you will be making mistakes throughout training, however you goal is to find gaps in your opponent's defenses and aim for those. This is the fundamental purpose of training. In addition training in Kenjutsu expands the chest and abdomen and promotes long life and an end to aging.

Chain and Sickle

The chain and sickle is used against swords, halberds, spears and other polearms. If you find an opening, wrap the chain around the opponent's weapon. There are innumerable situations where the chain and sickle can be used to your advantage and thus you should not fail to train this art.

Shuriken

Shuriken are a hidden weapon. Famous practitioners of this art can throw a Shuriken at a fly that has just landed on the ceiling and hit it. Or they can play a clever gambit and throw a shuriken at the hem of a guest rising to leave, thus stopping them in place. Most of these techniques are almost beyond human ability.

Jujutsu

Arresting Techniques

Jujutsu

This art is about not putting unnecessary power into your technique. You will have to receive an attack from left or right, in front or from behind and use that momentum to apply your technique. You follow along with the attacker's intent, then apply your own technique. Since this art uses the opponent's power to employ your technique it has been named Jujutsu.

There are many schools of Jujutsu, however the most important thing is to stay calm.

Torite
Arresting Techniques

The purpose of Torite is to take hold of and subdue a person, using a variety of techniques. Thus, you receive the attacker's first blow while maintaining an extreme sense of awareness that others may be trying to attack you. You force their chest to the ground in a way that takes the entire person into account.

Since Torite is a technique where you must leap in and seize a person, Jujutsu is employed with all its strategies and feints. You are suppressing the arms and legs as well as positioning yourself carefully around the opponent's stomach and chest. Torite requires that you adjust your approach according to the person you are arresting, however, in the end, the technique is about not allowing the person you seized to break free.

Long ago there were numerous famous practitioners who were able to subdue a man double their size. If you ever rise to become a famous practitioner yourself, there will be no situation that you can't solve with your arresting technique and it will offer you total protection.

Sumo Wrestlers

Sumo
Kakutei Contests of Strength (Sumo)
Ryoryoku Physical Strength (Sumo)

Nowadays Sumo is seen as a low-class sport, however it has a long history stretching back to ancient times. In 23 BC, the wrestler Nomino Sukune was ordered by the Emperor to fight Taima-no-Kehaya in the imperial palace. Nomino defeated Taima with a kick to his ribs and another kick to his back, killing him. The poet and politician Sugawara no Michizane (845 ~ 903,) who is revered as the Shinto god of learning, is a descendent of Nomino Sukune.

The strong fellows of today that do Sumo, have no trouble with the pace of training in their Dojo. They train diligently in Sumo because it is of great help on the battlefield. When a battle shifts to hand-to-hand unarmed combat, the benefits of Sumo are too numerous to count. On the other hand, Jujutsu and Torite are ineffective when both combatants are wearing armor. This is a pretty severe criticism, and there are of course exceptions.

It goes without saying that a person that reaches the pinnacle of the Sumo has full control over when to be hard and when to be soft, when to feint and when to launch their true attack. The first thing they do is toughen and harden their body. They also must learn to not make winning their primary motivation, rather they focus on the principle of "there is no possibility of me losing."

Further, if you are ever taught Sumo by a member of a Dojo or another person, you will learn the strengths and weaknesses of your body and spirit. It goes without saying you will learn when to apply strength and when to be flexible, when to feint and when to reveal your true intent. You will learn to understand your true self and learn how to use Kakegoe, a shout unifying body and spirit. You will develop an understanding about what your next move should be just as a good doctor can identify an illness.

All this applies not only to tournaments but in the training hall as well. Sumo wrestlers try to judge the color of the opponent's face as they battle. Even if they are unlucky in a match, it ends in a draw or they win, they do not use any illegal move. This is the way of the true victor in Sumo.

Teppo・Ju
Matchlocks

銃_ツ
鐵_レ
炮_ヲ

Teppo · Ju
Matchlocks

Teppo are officially called, Ju, or matchlocks. They are also known as "bird guns." People that are adept at shooting can shoot at a hundred different birds or beasts and score a hundred hits. Also, to show off, they will shoot a column nine times so that it resembles the pattern made by the nine luminaries, the seven visible planets plus comets and eclipses.

Experts can shoot the beak off a small bird, or shoot the foot off a bird. The greatest of these experts can shoot through both wings of a bird in flight, or hit a fish swimming in a pond. If you have not developed the ability to remain calm and focused, then you will never become a master shooter. This is an art you must not fail to learn.

Scroll of the 9 Luminaries from the Heian Era (794-1185)
Kuyō hiryaku 観筆九曜秘暦
The Secrets of the Nine Luminaries
By Sōkan 1125

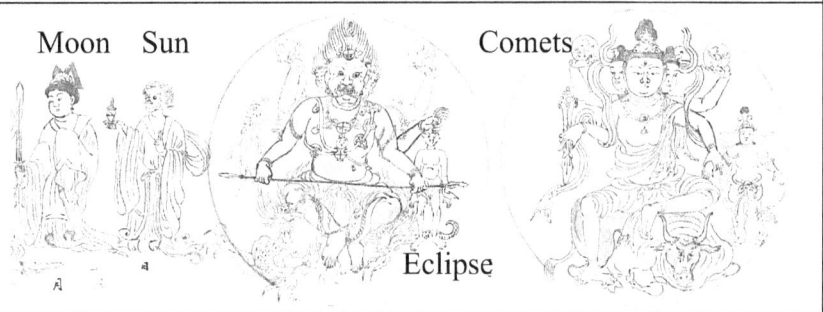

Moon Sun Comets

Eclipse

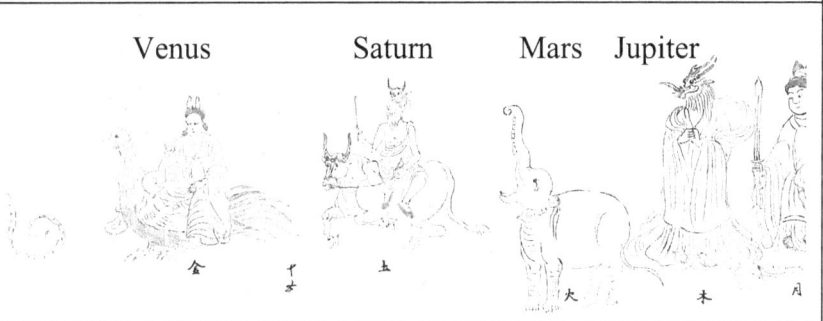

Venus Saturn Mars Jupiter

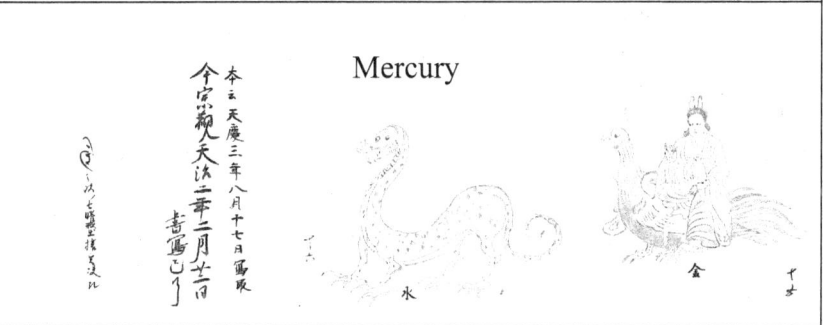

Mercury

Noh

Having studied all the previously mentioned arts to a greater or lesser degree, true Samurai will learn how to sing and dance Noh. This art has been enjoyed by Japanese since ancient times, thus performing it is nothing to be embarrassed about. Those watching find great enjoyment in the performances no matter what class, rich or poor. There is nothing more enjoyable than performing a dance in front of people.

Noh dances require you to have control over your spirit, abdomen and hips and infuse every part of your body with your will. In order for your voice to be clear, you need to be able to control your breathing. Thus the art of singing while dancing is good for the health of both young and old.

End